RHODODENDRONS

WITH
CAMELLIAS and MAGNOLIAS
2003

GW00370482

Royal
Horticultural
Society

Published in 2003 by
The Royal Horticultural Society,
80 Vincent Square, London SW1P 2PE

ISBN 1 902896 31 9

Edited for the RHS by Simon Maughan

Honorary Editor for the Rhododendron, Camellia and Magnolia Group
Philip Evans

Editorial Subcommittee
Maurice Foster
Rosemary Foster
Brian Wright

Opinions expressed by the authors are not necessarily those of
the Royal Horticultural Society

Printed by Page Bros, Norfolk

CONTENTS

COLOURED ILLUSTRATIONS

Front cover: Rhododendron glaucophyllum (see p.75) – third in a closely contested Class 10 at the Early Rhododendron Competition at Westminster, for Tregothnan; described as *R. glaucophyllum,* but possibly another species of subsect. Glauca *R. luteiflorum* (Photos Great Britain)
Back cover: (top) *Rhododendron* 'White Olympic Lady' ('Loderi King George' × *williamsii*) took first place for Brian Wright in Class 38 at the Main Rhododendron Competition at Westminster (Photos Great Britain);
Back cover: (bottom left) *Rhododendron* 'Naomi Paris', which won second prize for Ann Hooton in Class 37 at the Main Rhododendron Competition at Westminster, a name not in the list of the grex in 'The Rothschild Rhododendrons' (Phillips & Barber 1967) (Photos Great Britain);
Back cover: (bottom right) *Magnolia campbellii* 'Darjeeling' at Sherwood, the Devon Garden of Sir John and Lady Quicke photographed on a southwest branch visit (see p.63) (Dr G.B. Hargreaves)

Fig. 1: Yellow Magnolias at Herkenrode (Philippe de Spoelberch)
Fig. 2: Camellia 'Twighlight Glow' (C.R. Parkes)
Fig. 3: Camellia editheae (C.R. Parkes)
Fig. 4: Camellia chekiangoleosa (C.R. Parkes)
Fig. 5: Camellia × vernalis (C.R. Parkes)
Fig. 6: Camellia octopetala (C.R. Parkes)
Fig. 7: Camellia 'China Girl' (C.R. Parkes)
Fig. 8: Rhododendron 'Loderi Sir Edmund' FCC 1914 (Philip Evans)
Fig. 9: Rhododendron 'Loderi White Diamond' (Philip Evans)
Fig. 10: Azalea 'Pontica Chromatella' (Jim Inskip)
Fig. 11: Azalea 'Van Houtte Flore Pleno' (Jim Inskip)
Fig. 12: Azalea 'Standishii' (Jim Inskip)
Fig. 13: Azalea 'Bijou de Gentbrugge' (Jim Inskip)
Fig. 14: Magnolia stellata 'Goldstar' (Mike Robinson)
Fig. 15: Magnolia stellata 'Jane Platt' (Mike Robinson)
Fig. 16: Magnolia stellata (Jim Gardiner)
Fig. 17: Trillium chloropetalum white (Kevin Hughes)
Fig. 18: Lilium macklinae (Kevin Hughes)
Fig. 19: Erythronium 'White Beauty' (Kevin Hughes)
Fig. 20: Magnolia sieboldii (J.G. Rees)
Fig. 21: Rhododendron lindleyi (C. Waddington)
Fig. 22: Magnolia sprengeri var. *diva* (Dr G.B. Hargreave)
F*ig. 23: Rhododendron kendrickii (pankimense)* (Sir Ilay Campbell)
Fig. 24: Camellia 'Mattie Cole', *Camellia* 'Alba Simplex', *Camellia* 'Juno' (RHS)
Fig. 25: Camellia 'Mathotiana Rubra' (RHS)
Fig. 26: Camellia 'Lasca Beauty', *Camellia* 'Interval' and *Camellia* 'Edith Maggi' (RHS)
Fig. 27: Rhododendron tantastylum (Photos Great Britain)
Fig. 28: Rhododendron searsiae (Photos Great Britain)
Fig. 29: Garden at Sherwood, Devon (Hugh Dingle)

FOREWORD

MAURICE FOSTER

During the Group tour of North Germany last May we visited a garden not on the original itinerary, the historic Schlossgarten in Oldenburg, to the west of Bremen. Guided by Dr Eberhard Puehl, a garden historian, we were shown an original plant of *R.* 'Catawbiense Grandiflorum' purchased from the Waterer nursery in 1828, which was still going strong after almost 175 years. We saw many other old English hardy hybrids, mostly derived from *R. catawbiense, R. ponticum, R. maximum, R. caucasicum* and *R. arboreum,* clearly well suited to the relatively harsh winters of North Germany. Such plants were a feature not only of great estates and collections, but brightened the landscape everywhere in cottage gardens, farms and suburbs, as specimens, floral hedges and screens. In the Landwirtschaftskammer Weser-Ems gardens in Bad Zwischenahn, hardy hybrids were lined out like a reference library of living history, banked high with masses of flowers in many varied forms and colours. Our hosts' knowledge of, interest in and enthusiasm for the old English hardy hybrids, which thrive in their climate and soil, was impressive and stimulating. It was however tempered by the rather sad reflection that they had fallen so far out of fashion in the UK that many were being lost to cultivation.

A sense of history was thus much in evidence, but there was also a strong sense of current achievement and optimism for the future. Many of the eminent contemporaries in the development of the rhododendron in Germany – Hobbie, Hachmann, Bruns, for example – had drawn much of their inspiration from English collections and gardens and gone on to develop new generations of hybrids suited to their own conditions and tastes. An enormous range of compact hybrids has been developed for example by Hachmann father and son over the last 50 years. Their variety of form, foliage and spectacular flower illustrates this story of continuing development particularly well, and carries it on into the future.

Such success maintains the rhododendron as a popular garden plant that is widely enjoyed in North Germany, and the level of public interest in the genus is well illustrated by the remarkable attendance of over 93,000 people at the Westerstede rhododendron show, Rhodo 2002. This attendance is no less than 60 per cent of that at Chelsea – and to see only a single genus, the rhododendron. Incredibly, by contrast, it is now difficult to find a rhododendron at Chelsea, ostensibly squeezed out by a public in thrall to grasses and summer perennials.

Our visit to Germany leaves one with a sense of how important it is to acknowledge the value of our English 19th Century rhododendron legacy. It serves to confirm the importance of our own collection of Hardy Hybrids at Ramster and the need to continue to add to it potentially endangered remnants still to be found in old gardens everywhere – not only in the UK – where these historic plants still grow.

Cynthia Postan's article also points to the need to establish our Ramster collection as a "home for forgotten beauties". She recalls the Victorian heyday of the great 19th Century Surrey nurseries when, drawing fresh colour and form from crossing and recrossing with the introduction of fresh blood, growers continued to develop and preserve their popularity over decades. Like the 19th Century development of the gallica and hybrid perpetual roses in France, the hardy hybrid rhododendron characterised a whole era of horticultural development in the UK and the work of the Surrey nurserymen in particular, as well as a few amateurs, and helped to shape garden landscapes wherever rhododendrons could be grown.

In contrast to conditions in North Germany, where plant choice is limited principally by climate, Peter Cox's account of rhododendrons in Australia and New Zealand indicates the wide range of both species and hybrids that flourish there. Generally winters are benign, the climate more accommodating, and soils of enviable quality. The limiting factor is summer heat rather than winter cold and where this is moderated, conditions in certain areas are close to ideal. As an old forester said of parts of New Zealand – when you plant a tree, let go of the branches quickly, or you may be swung off your feet. In such conditions there is practically no limit to what can be grown, and in some spots the Loderi hybrids, interestingly researched and catalogued by Everard Daniel, are as much at home as in the Sussex woodland where they first flowered.

Further emphasising the international character of this issue in respect of all three genera, those attending the Vincent Square seminar on camellias last spring will be pleased to have a written version of Dr Clifford Parks' lecture on cold hardiness. It is packed with both scientific and practical information, with authoritative reference value and is of particular interest to members who would like to grow camellias in those parts of the world where winter conditions are more exacting.

I can report that the Group participated in a Wisley summer workshop, run jointly by IPPS and the Magnolia Society, on magnolia propagation. A paper on magnolias from seed emphasised the number of excellent named cultivars that had already been raised from open pollinated seed and the fact that, contrary to popular myth, on average, flowering was achieved in seven to eight years from sowing a variety of different cultivars and crosses – no longer than many other woody plants.

With an exceptional seed set on magnolias this year, at the time of writing there seems likely to be a wide choice of species and hybrids to be featured in the Group's Seed List. Members may be encouraged to acquire and sow a selection after reading Philippe de Spoelberch's appraisal of his collection of yellow magnolias in his arboretum at Herkenrode in Belgium. Looking ahead from this article, his collection of over one thousand magnolias, which includes the latest cultivars from across the world as well as his own hybrid seedlings, will be a highlight of the Group's tour of Belgian gardens in the spring. Philippe grows even more rhododendrons and our visit is likely to be something of a revelation to members taking part as to the scale and range of developments in both plants and gardens on the continent.

EDITORIAL

PHILIP EVANS

In recent years there has been concern, expressed in the Yearbook and elsewhere, about the low standing of rhododendrons in current gardening fashion. A stimulating antidote to all this was on offer in May last year, in the guise of 'Rhodo 02', a three-day conference at the Royal Botanic Gardens Edinburgh sponsored by the RBGE, the RHS, the Scottish Chapter of the ARS, and the Russell Trust, all of whom deserve our thanks. Entitled 'Rhododendrons in Science and Horticulture', and attended by some 200 rhododendron enthusiasts from around the world, the event demonstrated the intense and diverse interest this complex genus inspires in many different disciplines. Several papers revealed the surprisingly wide role of the genus in scientific research. Kathy Kron explained how rhododendron molecular data, from the chloroplast and nuclear genomes, can now be used to reassess evolutionary relationships within the genus; while, later, Gillian Brown demonstrated more specifically a phylogeny of rhododendron subsect vireya, produced from chloroplast DNA. Then, David Rankin spoke of the application of chemical analysis in resolving taxonomic problems, in particular the analysis of the chemical compounds in rhododendron leaf waxes, using which he has identified natural hybrids amongst varieties of subsection taliensia. Eric Nilson explained how rhododendron's geographic and climatic

diversity, especially of subsect vireya, makes it an ideal system for identifying and studying the adaptive traits of plants. Rajeev Avora described how he had used rhododendron for his genetic and physiological research into plant cold hardiness, while George Dixon told us something of the biology of cold hardiness in rhododendrons themselves.

For most, the horticultural aspects of rhododendron are more familiar territory, and here the range was wide indeed. We heard Michael Thomley describe his inspirational restoration of the celebrated Scottish garden Glenarn, Michael Lear and Rachel Martin on cataloguing the Exbury collection, Jim Gardiner on rhododendrons at Wisley, and Graham Smith on the great New Zealand garden Pukeiti. We heard from David Paterson and Dr Li DeZhu about the creation of a pioneer Botanic Garden at Lijiang, in the very Chinese rhododendron heartland. We heard also from two experienced contemporary plant hunters Kenneth Cox and Steve Hootman, about the Tsangpo Gorge of Tibet and the Dulong valley between Burma and China, two only partly explored rhododendron collecting areas; from Rebecca Pradhan on the wild rhododendrons of Bhutan, and David Binney on the vireyas of Sulawesi. Cultural subjects well explored were powdery mildew, biological control of weeds, and rhododendron husbandry and hygiene. We even heard, from of all people a professional conservationist, Ian Rotherham, an eloquent defence of a place in our landscape for that maligned beauty, *R. ponticum.*

This summary falls short of mentioning all the excellent papers presented, but gives some idea of what a broad tapestry was woven, producing a compound profile of genus *Rhododendron* and its place in the world of this new millennium. Congratulations to Dr George Argent and his team at the RBGE for the concept and the organisation.

Whilst in Edinburgh one took the opportunity to walk around the immaculate Royal Botanic Gardens and see something of their great rhododendron collection – a specimen of the white *R. augustinii* subsp. *hardyi* particularly impressed. Also noted was the imaginative underplanting, including groups of trillium in flower. In the wild one can witness the wide variety of plants woody, herbaceous ands bulbous, with which rhododendrons associate –

nature's reminder of what can be attempted in the garden. Companion planting and plant associations are valuable subjects for treatment in the Yearbook, and featured in this issue is an excellent article by Kevin Hughes, an expert on trilliums, on bulbous plants for association with rhododendrons and camellias.

Acknowledgement should be made to the contribution of Karen Wilson as the RHS editor involved in the production of the Yearbook, from 1996 until she left the RHS at the end of last year. Her work and support each year in converting a ring binder of text with supporting disks and photos, into the quality finished article that eventually emerges from the printer, has been much appreciated. Thanks are also due to all the contributors to this issue, in particular those several members who produced reports on individual gardens visited on the two garden tours.

THE FLOWERING AND DEMISE OF
RHODODENDRON PANKIMENSE

HUGH DINGLE

In his book *Plant Hunter's Paradise*, which describes his 1931 trip to the Adung Valley in Northern Burma, Frank Kingdon-Ward makes numerous references to *R. pankimense*, and one is surprised when *R. pankimense* fails to appear in Appendix IV at the end of the book, which includes 34 Numbers of *Rhododendron* collections from that expedition.

Kingdon-Ward serialised 45 articles for *The Gardeners' Chronicle* describing the trip, and they were published in the issues from April 1932 to December 1933. Despite his many references to *R. pankimense* in *Plant Hunter's Paradise*, there are none in *The Gardeners' Chronicle*. But there are passages where Book and Chronicle make parallel observations, identifying *R. pankimense* of the book with *R. tanastylum*.

Plant Hunter's Paradise
p. 117, at Tahawndam.
  'Much smaller than *R. magnificum*, but equally common, was the rosy crimson *R. pankimense*. This was in bud when we first arrived, but not in bloom. It first opened its flowers during the third week of February, …'

The Gardeners' Chronicle
August 27, 1932
  'There was a small-leafed 'Irroratum' already in crimson bud – evidently *R. tanastylum*; and so it

proved to be, when, ten days later, it opened its first flowers. (KW 9236)'

Plant Hunter's Paradise
p 144.
  'On March 2nd it snowed again at Base Camp. … This depression, however, did not prevent the peach blossom from opening, nor did it injure the shrill yellow flowers of *Rhododendron seinghkuense*. But a large bush of purple *R. pankimense* in full bloom close to our camp was a sorry spectacle of sagging and shattered flowers.'

The Gardeners' Chronicle
October 8, 1932
  'The snowstorm of March 2nd ruined the flowering trees of *Rhododendron tanastylum* by the river, but did not prevent *R. seinghkuense* and the village peach trees from breaking into blossom.'

Plant Hunter's Paradise
p. 159
  'At the top we came out on to steep acres of scorched grazing land, fiercely hot… We reached the bothy, between two patches of forest, vividly coloured with rhododendrons. We were… about 8000 feet above sea level. The first thing that struck me was that here grew many of the same trees which we had already seen along the river bank. Only they flowered later. There were pure stands of *Rhododendron*

pankimense: the fringe of the forest where it peeped over the steep ridge was splendidly purple with its variable blooms.'

The Gardeners' Chronicle
October 8, 1932

'We… came out on to… thousands of acres of dry, scorched grazing land… a slanting path… at an altitude of 8,000 feet… The first thing we noticed was that *Rhododendron tanastylum*, which was quite over in the valley, was in full bloom up here, and it was one of the commonest species. It varied a good deal in colour, but the prevailing shade was a dark cherry crimson.'

One can be forgiven for deducing that Kingdon-Ward saw plants he called *R. pankimense* in 1931, but in 1932 had second thoughts, and recognised them as *R. tanastylum*. But first, what is the derivation of the name *pankimense*?

It refers to a mountain pass, the Pankim La, in the Balipara Frontier Tract in Arunachal Pradesh, hard against the eastern border of Bhutan. It features foothills and southern ranges of the Eastern Himalaya, to the north of the Brahmaputra river. Kingdon-Ward crossed the pass in May 1935 on his way up to Tibet, and is lyrical about the country revealed to him:

Journal of the Royal Central Asian Society
1939

'The sun was shining in a beautiful blue sky. Gone was the white mist which curled dismally amongst the trees on the south side, gone too the dense jungle with its wrappings of moss. Blue pines towered up amongst vivid green oaks, spring flowers carpeted the earth, and below were cultivated fields. The whole scene reminded one irresistibly of England in spring.'

Here, Kingdon-Ward collected his Number KW 11378.

The Gardeners' Chronicle
10 October 1936

'On May 3 we crossed the pass [Pankim La] over the outer range at 10,000 feet. At the summit were many Rhododendrons, forming dense thickets. Here, with *Rhododendron arboreum*, grew a new species, closely allied to *R. tanastylum*, but with purple instead of crimson flowers. *R. tanastylum* is a Burmese, not a Sikkim species.'

The Gardeners' Chronicle
24 October 1936

'… we found the top of the range covered with forest similar to that already described for the Pankim La… the same Rhododendrons as before… This *R. pankimense* has been separated from *R. tanastylum*, with which I identified it, by Dr. J. M. Cowan; there are minor botanical differences, besides the important one of flower colour for the collector gardener. *R. pankimense* is, I think, likely to be hardier than *R. tanastylum*.'

In Notes from the Royal Botanic Garden Edinburgh of 1936, Cowan & Ward published their account of *R. pankimense*, Sp. nov., ("Corolla crimson marked with numerous darker spots") based on KW 11378. The article goes on to tell how *R. pankimense* differs from the closely related *R. kendrickii* (in leaf and truss), *R. tanastylum* (in leaf and ovary) and *R. ramsdenianum* (in leaf, corolla and ovary).

The designation stood for many years and is listed in the 1967 Rhododendron Handbook, but it failed to survive Dr Chamberlain's wind of change of 1980/82, when KW 11378 was identified as *R. kendrickii*; a species that had been collected from Balipara or from adjacent Bhutan by

William Griffith in 1838, Booth in 1849 and by R. E. Cooper in 1915.

Sir Ilay Campbell writes that there are at Crarae three plants that used to be labelled *R. pankimense*, none with a collector's number, of which two were later identified as *R. anthosphaerum*, and one as *R. kendrickii* (See Fig.23). A fourth plant proved to be *R. ramsdenianum*, and won prizes under that name, but has since died.

Reading *Plant Hunter's Paradise* one is transported to the Adung Valley in 1931, and as *R. pankimense* features quite largely one wonders what plant that is. Confusion follows with the realisation that in May 1935, Kingdon-Ward crossed the Pankim La for the first time! Why, "in 1931", had he called rhododendrons in the Adung Valley after the Pankim La some 550km to the west, when he had never been there? And of course the most obvious of simple answers is – *Plant Hunter's Paradise* was not published until 1937. Home from the Pankim La, writing or revising, Kingdon-Ward must have considered the plants he had seen in the Adung Valley in 1931 more akin to his new 'Irroratum', *R. pankimense*, than to *R. tanastylum*. This appears to have been a short-lived opinion, as in Appendix IV to the book KW 9236 is identified as *R. tanastylum*, and at no time has that Number been given a different name. I believe it true to say that for '*R. pankimense*' read '*R. kendrickii*' unless you are reading *Plant Hunter's Paradise*.

In *Assam Adventure*, Kingdon-Ward's description of the 1935 journey published in 1941, the crossing of the Pankim La is not described; the book opens with the author in Shergaon, the first village north of the pass. There is only the briefest reference to *R. pankimense*, where he noted it in August in Tibet in the valley of the river Yigrong, a tributary of the Tsangpo (p.180). This observation does not tally with any KW Number.

Peter Cox, who has seen all three in the wild, confirms the great difficulty in distinguishing between *R. tanastylum*, *R. kendrickii* and *R. ramsdenianum*. True *R. tanastylum* is extremely rare in cultivation, but a specimen has been so identified in the Clyne Castle collection.

My grateful thanks Sir Ilay Campbell for the provision of trusses and photographs of *R. pankimense/kendrickii* at Crarae (see Fig.23), and to Peter Cox for his help and guidance.

References

KINGDON-WARD, F (1937). *Plant Hunter's Paradise*. Jonathan Cape, London.

KINGDON-WARD, F (1941). *Assam Adventure*. Jonathan Cape, London.

KINGDON-WARD, F (1932). Mr F. Kingdon-Ward's 11th Expedition in Asia – XI. *The Gardeners' Chronicle* 3.Ser. XCII 158–160.

KINGDON-WARD, F (1932). Mr F. Kingdon-Ward's 11th Expedition in Asia – XIV. *The Gardeners' Chronicle* 3.Ser. XCII: 266–267.

KINGDON-WARD, F (1939). The Assam Himalaya: Travels in Balipara – II. *Journal of the Royal Central Asian Society* 26: 309–324.

KINGDON-WARD, F (1936). Mr F. Kingdon-Ward's 13th Expedition in Asia: Journey to Tibet – I. *The Gardeners' Chronicle* 3.Ser. C: 268–269.

KINGDON-WARD, F (1936). Mr F. Kingdon-Ward's 13th Expedition in Asia: Journey to Tibet – II. *The Gardeners' Chronicle* 3.Ser. C: 302–304.

COWAN & KINGDON-WARD (1936). Rhododendron pankimense. *Notes from the RBG Edinburgh* 19: 180–182.

Hugh Dingle is a member of the Group and lives in Jersey

Yellow Magnolias at Herkenrode and Arboretum Wespelaar[1]

Philippe de Spoelberch

Our Editor managed to push me into writing these notes although we are far from having all the yellow-flowering magnolias that are found in the trade. It is therefore much too early to propose any kind of evaluation. Worse even, we have raised many seedlings from crosses made by the late Dr August Kehr. The result is more plants to evaluate and never-ending rankings. I had hoped to be able to postpone this paper as most yellow magnolia had been hit by frost this year (2002) in the bud. After a very mild winter and very early spring, frost finally came and the season was ruined. All of the classical yellows were a disaster. I hope that the reader will accept these notes as a base for discussion and further comments.

Flowering dates

I had to go back to my 2000 figures to find relevant flowering data. The taxa hereunder have been in the collection for several years and we were able to reach some conclusions. The table below has been taken from a major study of the flowering of magnolia (some 300 taxa). Many of the newer cultivars have not been included because they had not flowered significantly for sufficient years.

These were the results for the taxa studied. All magnolia in the collection were evaluated every three days and it was determined if they were "starting" (tepals just visible out of the bud), "peak" (more than one-third of flowers well open), or "end" (no tepals left on the plant).

Name of Magnolia	Flowering dates (day in year, 2000)			
	start	peak	end	total
M. 'Petit Chicon' (*acuminata* × *denudata*)	87	96	117	30
M. 'Banana Split' [('Woodsman' × 'Lennei') × 'Elizabeth']	99	108	129	30
M. 'Carlos' (*acuminata* var. *subcordata* × *denudata*)	99	108	126	27
M. 'Elizabeth' (*acuminata* × *denudata*)	96	108	132	36
M. 'Limelight' (*acuminata* × 'Big Pink')	87	108	129	42
M. 'Sundance' (*acuminata* × *denudata*)	96	108	129	33
M. 'Yellow Fever' (*acuminata* × *denudata*)	93	108	129	36
M. 'Yellow Lantern' (*acuminata* var. *subcordata* × 'Big Pink')	93	108	132	39
M. (*acuminata* × *cylindrica*)	108	117	129	21
M. (*acuminata* × 'Norman Gould')	111	117	132	21
M. 'Yellow Bird' (*acuminata* × 'Evamaria')	111	117	132	21
M. acuminata 'Miss Honeybee' seedling	117	120	132	15
M. 'Daphne' ('Miss Honeybee' × 'Gold Crown')	117	120	139	22
M. acuminata var. *subcordata*	117	123	139	22
M. acuminata 'Seiju'	117	126	151	34

The earliest of all, **'Petit Chicon'** (*M. acuminata × denudata*), is a selection from the garden of Karl E. Flink in Sweden (reference Bjuv 1636), cuttings of which I took there in June of 1987. The cross was probably made by Phil Savage. It has proven to be so constantly effective and charming that it has been propagated for several years. It flowered nine days earlier than 'Elizabeth', on the 87th day (27 March 2001) until 117th day (26 May) for a total of 30 days. Three cuttings of 'Petit Chicon' have been grown here for 13 years. They never fail to attract attention. The main interest of the taxon is its early flowering, well before any leaves, and the hardy, well-structured small flowers. They are pale yellow, open completely, and remain star like for several days before falling off.[2]

The next batch of yellow magnolia follows ten days later with 'Elizabeth', 'Sundance' and 'Yellow Fever', all crosses of *M. acuminata × denudata*. **'Elizabeth'** is still one of the best for regularity and hardiness. Never disappointing even when its flowers get hit by some frost. It is not as deeply yellow every year, and plants held in the heat of a greenhouse seem to be darker yellow. Like all the *denudata* crosses, it fades to white as the flower opens. The story of this cross is well known.[3] Clearly, the miserable weather of Belgium does not suit these plants. If 'Elizabeth' is reasonably hardy, **'Yellow Fever'** on the other hand, will often be damaged by spring frost. Consequently, these would-be trees become stunted and flowers are much reduced in size. On the other hand, plants of that cross seen in Northern Italy and Ticino province of Switzerland are glorious. **'Sundance'** should be grown under the canopy of pine trees, not in the open. It is the palest of the so-called yellow magnolia, especially in a cool climate. If there is any sunshine and warmth, the flowers will open up completely for a time before falling. The totally reflexed tepals are a delight. **'Carlos'** is a good selection (not registered) which is deeper in colour. **'Fei Huang'** (syn. **'Yellow River'**), a recent introduction possibly from China via Holland, does not show much difference from 'Elizabeth', possibly an improvement in flower, but it is much too early to say if this will be such a hardy and vigorous plant.

From another cross comes **'Limelight'** (*acuminata × 'Big Pink'*), flowering later than the previous cultivars; the flowers of 'Limelight' are also much bigger and sickle shaped, bending away form the light (as with the "Girls"). Phil Savage often used 'Big Pink' (then called *M. soulangeana* 'Alexandrina Japanese Form') in his crosses. The tepals of 'Limelight' do not open flat but fall suddenly from a closed position. This is nevertheless a good yellow both for its size and depth of colour. It is slightly green on the base of the outer tepals. **'Yellow Lantern'** (*M. acuminata* var. *subcordata × 'Big Pink'*) got through the frost in 2002 but is not as floriferous as 'Limelight' born of the same parents.

M. acuminata was crossed by August Kehr with *M. cylindrica* (probably 'Pegasus') and *M. kobus* 'Norman Gould'. Several seedlings have been raised and allowed to prosper. These could hardly be called yellow although they flower at the same time as the other so-called yellows. From a distance they have a curious yellow-green look reminiscent of lemon ice cream; these are big trees and have retained the growth habit of *M. acuminata*. They have great charm and also get voted good points by visitors. **'Gold Star'** is another cross in this section, this time with *M. stellata* providing for a charming, neat, frost-resistant, first-class flower of a distinct pale yellow. It is, once again, interesting to note how easily this big American tree will hybridise with all sections of magnolia.

The later-flowering yellow magnolia have strong contributions from *M. acuminata* var. *subcordata*, the southern form of the cucumber tree. Of course, they will tend to flower with the leaves. **'Yellow Bird'** (*M. acuminata* × *brooklynensis* 'Evamaria') is a well-known cultivar in this group. This is a true yellow, which unfortunately is not very hardy, in the open, in Belgium. It has been regularly hit by late spring frosts which have damaged the stem. It should probably be grown under the canopy of pine trees. It flowers with the leaves, providing for a good combination of fresh green and deep yellow. In our climate and on old plants, the leaves tend to wrap around the flowers and hide them. It is one of the latest yellows and will bloom right into the time when the *Rhytidospermum* will start to flower. Has anyone tried that cross?

New trials from August Kehr crosses

Some 127 seedlings were raised from crosses made in 1991 by August Kehr. Some have been flowering at Arboretum Wespelaar where they were eventually planted out. A few are producing spectacular flowers. The deepest yellows have been achieved in crosses using *M. acuminata* var. *subcordata* 'Miss Honeybee'. Good seedlings from the following crosses have been raised, a few have been named:

- ('Miss Honeybee' × 'Gold Crown'): **'Daphne'** and **'Greenbee'**, good deep yellow held up at the end of branches.
- ('Miss Honeybee' × 'Elizabeth'): of which one named selection, **'Honey Liz'** with huge floppy deep yellow flowers on an upright tree.

- ('Miss Honeybee' × 'Golden Glow'): has produced very unstable plants and is definitely not a good cross! Small yellow flowers have appeared on some seedlings, but these are not very hardy.
- (*M. acuminata* × 'Elizabeth'): a tree-like seedling of very vigorous habit with large yellow flowers; this is the same cross as 'Lois'.
- ('Yellow Bird' × 'Sundance'): one seedling with small but well-filled flowers, good deep yellow fading to fawn with traces of pink.
- [('Woodsman' × 'Lennei') × 'Elizabeth']: of which, **'Banana Split'** and **'Green Snow'** with huge floppy flowers, with tepals showing various shades of white, green, yellow and pink!

M. × *brooklynensis* 'Woodsman' was not a very good parent; most seedlings have been cut; they produced small brownish flowers of no significance: *M.* [('Woodsman' × 'Lennei') × ('Woodsman' × 'Sundance')] and *M.* ('Woodsman' × 'Lennei').

Hopefully everyone will find some pleasure in these great crosses of Augie Kehr. He continued to make crosses until his last days, and we must all be grateful for his efforts and perspicacity. Not all crosses have yielded good siblings, but many of his late yellow crosses will be here to stay.

The last yellow magnolia to flower with us, are other unnamed *M. acuminata* var. *subcordata*. Even if flowers are small and soon break open, these are the good deep yellow which will eventually be bred into hardier plants with bigger flowers and possible some doubles. We have continued to cross these and the August Kehr hybrids and will have to wait another eight years to see the result!

Untested cultivars

We should also have a chance to report on other good yellows that have been recommended and have not yet had a chance to flower here. Anyone wanting to join the evaluation should not fail to try these too: in particular 'Lois' a backcross of 'Elizabeth' with *M. acuminata*, of which Maurice Foster says:

> "It is the best yellow we grow. It is still effective in the landscape in mid-May as, although leafing out, the flowers are held clear of the leaves and are still visible to colour the tree. It remains the best-shaped balanced flower of pleasing form, with 9 quite broad overlapping tepals and none of the 'gappy' and twisted look of *M. acuminata*. It is a good primrose and does not fade and the flowers fall before they discolor."

We have not been able to flower **'Butterflies'**. Against a background of negative comments, I can only say that, having seen the mother plant in Phil Savage's garden in Detroit, I will continue to wait. Maurice Foster again has an interesting comment in reply to my query:

> "We were about to take the saw to our two plants as it seemed to have little going for it, with narrow twisted tepals and a spreading habit. But this year it must have been in flower for as long as your 'Limelight'. It is genuinely precocious and has a good display well before any other yellow, and is a good colour."

With time, most of these new cultivars will disappear; I must admit that I have a tremendous pleasure cutting uninteresting crosses, but I suppose that one never cuts enough. A selection that looks gorgeous one year may be disappointing during the next two seasons. And so, one remains on the conservative side. A group of Scandinavian visitors fell in love with *M. acuminata* × 'Norman Gould' and also *M. acuminata* × *cylindrica,* which they thought would be hardy under their Nordic climate. So maybe I was right to let them live. But in the meantime small seedlings become huge trees and their branches start to touch, and one is soon in a wood, maybe a forest, with a few flowers way up, out of reach…

[1] Arboretum Wespelaar is located in Belgium, to the north of Brussels. Organised as a private foundation, it has taken over responsibility for the development and care of some 15ha of botanical collections, previously planted as an extension of the garden at Herkenrode. Arboretum Wespelaar manages the inventory of botanical collections in several gardens of the de Spoelberch family in Wespelaar, Belgium. The collection, spread over some 50ha of land, comprises 10,500 living accessions of woody species of which 1067 were living magnolias at the end of 2001.

[2] The name 'Petit Chicon' has been given as the result of a spontaneous comment by my daughter as to the fact that it resembles a small endive as they are grown in Belgium.

[3] see Jim Gardiner. *Magnolias* (2000), p.210. Timber Press.

Vicomte Philippe de Spoelberch is a Belgian member of the Group. He is president of the Belgian Dendrology Society, a Council Member of the International Dendrology Society and a Board Member of The Magnolia Society

Rhododendron 'Loderi' How Distinct are the Different Clones?

Everard Daniel

It is now 100 years since Sir Edmund Loder made that most famous of crosses between *R. fortunei* and *R. griffithianum*, and this centenary was celebrated (in 2001) at Leonardslee. Of course, the cross had been made before and called *R.* × *kewense*, but it is always said that the results were definitely inferior and it is good that the taxonomists have allowed the later name to be used, when the earlier would normally take precedence.

To produce this world-famous cross, Leonardslee teamed up with Col. Godman at South Lodge, on the other side of the A281, as he had a particularly fine form of *R. griffithianum* growing under glass. This plant is, alas, long-since lost, although there are other plants of this species still growing there, in the gardens of what is now a hotel. I often wondered whether these are from the same batch of seed as that famous parent. They seem perfectly hardy there, despite the tender reputation that this species has. It is recorded that the cross was made three times, with pollen being carried across the road in both directions but that the best results came from *R. griffithianum* pollen onto *R. fortunei*, which was done twice. The reverse cross produced flowers that were much like *R. fortunei*; was this chance or could there be a genetic reason?

Apparently, the cross was first made in 1901, and the first flowers were seen in 1907, probably on 'Diamond', now known as 'White Diamond'. Robin Loder, the great grandson of Sir Edmund Loder and the present owner of Leonardslee, is certain that the best clones come from this first batch. 'Diamond' and 'Pink Diamond' were first to be shown and both were awarded the FCC, in 1914. 'King George' had to wait for the FCC until 1970.

Quite a number of different clones have been registered and although it is the name of 'King George' that everyone knows, I have long felt that, as they are all closely related and indeed many are 'sisters', it would be a braver man than me that would walk up to a plant and claim to identify the clone! The differences are very slight, and one could easily think two trusses are from different clones when in fact they came from opposite sides of the same plant. I certainly feel that the descriptions one generally reads are inadequate for positive identification. As they are so similar and so popular, and therefore widely propagated and planted all over the world, it is inevitable that they have become confused and so many plants are grown under the wrong name.

It has been a privilege to have spent several idyllic evenings at Leonardslee in 2001 and

Fig. 1: Yellow Magnolias at Herkenrode (see p.12), from left to right: Top row: 'Elizabeth', 'Green Bee', sister of 'Green Bee'. 2nd row: 'Honey Beth', 'Honey Crown', 'Honey Liz'. 3rd row: M. acuminata × 'Norman Gould', 'Banana Split', ('Woodsman × 'Lennei') × 'Elizabeth'. Bottom row: M. acuminata × 'Elizabeth', 'Woodsman'× 'Lennei', 'Yellow Dance'.

Winter Tolerance in Canellias:
Fig. 2 (left): Camellia *'Twighlight Glow' (see p.20).*
Fig. 3 (above): Camellia editheae, *a striking variety*
with beautiful foliage and heat-resisting flowers
(see p.22). Fig. 4 (below): Camellia chekiangoleosa, *a close relative of* C. japonica *(see p.21).*

Winter tolerance in Camellias:
Fig. 5 (left): Camellia × vernalis, *a cross between* C. sasanqua *and* C. japonica *(see p.22).*
Fig. 6 (above): Camellia octopetala *(see p.21).*
Fig. 7 (below): Camellia *'China Girl'* – C. sasanqua × C. reticulata *(see p.22).*

Fig. 8 (above): Rhododendron 'Loderi Sir Edmund' FCC 1914 at Leonardslee, showing pink coloration richest and most persistent near petal edge. Note also little or no throat markings and purple petiole (see p.17). *Fig. 9 (left):* Rhododendron 'Loderi White Diamond' at Leonardslee, showing how the pink buds open to pure white flowers with throat markings. The first Loderi to flower in 1907 (see p.16).

2002 looking at as many of the original plants as I could, and also at younger plants, especially in the Coronation Garden there, where a collection was planted in 1953. I have also been able to study the plants at Wisley and Windsor. One hopes that we can rely on the original plants to be correctly labelled, but probably not on any other, even in their home garden. I looked for a truss in which the last flower was nearly fully expanded and then examined the oldest flower in that truss, noting:

1. the size
2. the colour of the petals
3. whether there was any colour in the veins
4. the presence of any markings in the throat

The general pattern is that they nearly all open from pink buds but rapidly fade to white and I was surprised that even the ones that I had thought of as pinker were in fact nearly pure white by this stage. The colour lasts longest in the veins, particularly towards the outer edges of the petals, and this does seem to be a useful diagnostic character, as do the throat markings. None of them show more than two or three thin lines of small spots and speckles, which are confined to the throat and lead upwards for perhaps one-third of the length of the petal. They do not show the pronounced markings that one sees in some of their offspring, such as 'Avalanche' and 'Albatross'. I measured the width from the tip of one lobe to the tip of the opposite; I did not stretch or flatten it. The range was 12–14.5cm; most are between 13–14cm. The clones seem all equally scented. So, can one be definite in identification? I feel that I still cannot, but that certain patterns have emerged that can be used to group the clones, which I show in Table 1. At this point, a word of caution in that these observations were made in one place and in two seasons and that in different conditions, especially temper-

ature, each clone might appear quite differently. Warmer conditions would quite possibly make the flowers open faster and so be smaller and fade faster. Also 2001 was an exceptionally late season, with the Loderis opening between two and three weeks later than usual.

So is 'King George' the one that everyone should have, or is it just that that is the name everyone can remember? I incline to the latter view, although the 'King George' were particularly floriferous in 2001. At 14cm, it is of average size and is certainly not the largest, that honour going to 'Sir Edmund' at 15cm. It is the purest white, having virtually no throat markings. The scent is outstanding – just like all the others!

I have become particularly taken with 'Sir Edmund' as it was heavily laden with large (14–15cm) flowers, and is very much the pinkest of the originals, with definite pink veins, and it is the only one to really retain the colour and appear pink in the landscape. But it is still only a pale pink. 'Pink Diamond' rivals it, although smaller and the late Sir Giles Loder thought it the darkest. The others that are reputedly pink, such as 'Pink Coral', 'Pink Topaz', 'Venus' and 'Princess Marina', are really only pink for a short period as they open. However, there are real pinks in the subsequent generations: 'Georgette' is a rich pink that fades only slowly in the semi-shade and 'Irene Stead' from New Zealand is very similar. 'Sir Edmund', 'Patience' and 'Venus' are also slightly different in that they open a few days later, and 'Gamechick' seems to be regularly about a week later than most, so is of value.

Controversially, Bean tells us that the original plant of 'Venus' was at Exbury, suggesting it is not one of the 1901 crossing. Neither is 'Princess Marina', which is 'King George' × 'Sir Edmund'; this clone is a dis-

Colour	Throat markings R=red dots G=green dots	Slight throat marking	Throat markings absent or only very faint
White	'White Diamond' (R) 'Gamechick' (G)	'Sir Joseph Hooker' (R+G) *#'Helen' (R)	'King George' **'Dairymaid'
Blush, ie very nearly white	'Venus' (R) 'Pink Coral' (R+G) *'Patience' (R+G) 'Pink Diamond' (R+G)	'Loderi South Lodge' (not registered, but propagated by Alan Clark) **'Fairyland' (R) *'Fairy Queen' (R) *'Spearmint' (R) ***'White Pearl' (G)	'Princess Marina'
Pale Pink	**'Pink Topaz' (G)	'Sir Edmund' (G)	Another 'South Lodge' form
Pink	'Georgette' (R)		

Table 1 *Loderi Clones by Colour Group*   * = *From plant in the Coronation Garden, Leonardslee*
** = *From plant in the RHS Garden Wisley, Surrey*   *** = *From plant in the Savill Gardens, Windsor*

tinctive shell pink with *paler* edges. Another distinctive form is 'Dairymaid' (as seen at Wisley) – the palest in bud, showing little or no pink colouring, and opening to milky white (Sir Giles thought it greenish).

There are several clones that are relatively little known but are just as valuable. 'Spearmint' has recently been re-discovered in the Coronation Garden at Leonardslee growing near 'Fairy Queen'. Millais mentions a clone called 'Queen Mary', who was of course the wife of 'King George', but this clone is long since lost and forgotten at Leonardslee. 'Pretty Polly' may well have also died out. Has anyone ever seen either? 'Stag's Head' grows elsewhere and should soon return. 'Titan' was raised by Reuthe's Nursery at Sevenoaks in England and 'Olga' ('Pink Diamond' × 'King George') by Brandt in the USA. 'Julie' is well known as the cream form, and is very different from the rest; her origin remains rather a mystery, although Bean says she was raised at Lord Swathling's Townhill Park, Hampshire from two Loderi parents. There are only two quite young plants that are probably of this clone at Leonardslee. As 'Julie' lacks the characteristic purple leaf stalk (petiole) that Loderi inherits from *R. fortunei* and the flowers are smaller

and more tubular, one must question the given parentage. South Lodge has forms that seem slightly different, so they are likely to be other, unnamed seedlings of this most distinguished of hybrids, and there seem to be such seedlings in many Sussex gardens, no doubt distributed from Leonardslee. Several were named from The High Beeches (at that time owned by others of the Loder family), and these tend to be named after racehorses.

References

LODER, Sir Giles (1951). *Rhododendron Yearbook*. Royal Horticultural Society. (Reprinted in current Loder Plants catalogue and online at www.rhododendrons.com).

BEAN, W.J. (1980). *Trees and shrubs hardy in the British Isles*. John Murray.

MILIAIS, J.G. (1918). *Rhododendron and the various hybrids*. Longmans, Green, London.

SALLEY H. & GREER H. (1992). *Rhododendron hybrids* 2nd Edn. Batsford, London.

Everard Daniel is a member of the southeast branch of the Group

Clonal Name	Width (cm)	Colour					Throat Spots					Comments
		Pink	Pale Pink	Blush	White	Pink Veining	Red	Faint Red	Green	Faint Green	None	
'Dairymaid'**					y					y		pale buds and petioles
'Fairyland'**			y			y	y					
'Fairy Queen'*			y							y		smaller and poorer
'Gamechick'					y				y			one week later flowering
'Georgette'		y				y	y					proper pink
'Hammerkop'												at High Beeches, 1935
'Helen'***			y				y					small flower, paler petiole
'Irene Stead'***		y										proper pink
'Julie'												yellowish cream
'King George'	14				y					y	y	most floriferous
'Olga'												
'Patience'*	13		y				y		y			poorer; later
'Pearly Queen'												
'Pink Coral'	13		y				y					most heavily marked
'Pink Diamond'	13		y				y	y	y	y		marks very variable
'Pink Topaz'**				y	y				y			
'Pretty Polly'												
'Princess Marina'			y								y	shell pink paler edge
'Queen Mary'												
'Sir Edmund'	15	y				y				y	y	later
'Sir Joseph Hooker'	14				y			y		y		red marks persist later and floriferous
'South Lodge'	14.1		y			y				y	y	Possibly = 'Sir Edmund'
'Spearmint'			y					y				
'Superlative'												
'Stag's Head'												
'Titan'												
'Venus'	15		y				y					2 or 3 spot rows
'White Diamond'	13.5				y		y			y		
'White Pearl'**			y							y		name questionable

Table 2   *A List of all the Loderi Clones Known to Me.*
Results not recorded for clones where I have not yet been able to examine flowers at the correct age.
See Table 1 for clonal name key.

Winter Tolerance in Camellias

Clifford R. Parks

Research trips to import hardy *Camellia* stocks were initiated about 50 years ago. Expeditions were made to colder parts of Japan to locate and collect cold-resistant camellias. Materials were imported from northeastern Japan and the high snowfall zone on Honshu Island next to the Sea of Japan. Accessions from northeastern Japan have proven to be cold resistant. However, in field trials, the camellias from the high snowfall zone along the Sea of Japan did not demonstrate cold resistance in the United States. About 20 years later, *C. japonica* was collected from islands off the western coast of Korea near the 38th parallel. The hardiness of the accessions from northeastern Japan and Korea are probably similar, but the Korean collections have been used much more extensively in breeding, particularly in recent years.

While the work on combining the wild-collected, hardy accession of *C. japonica* with garden varieties represents the first effort to develop hardier cultivars through plant breeding, gardeners have been observing and recording hardiness of their garden varieties long before the trips to Japan and Korea. Observations on survival and flowering of cultivars were made in the colder areas where camellias were cultivated, particularly around Washington, DC and adjacent areas. The list of hardy cultivars developed by gardeners and nurserymen became the basis for cultivation in the colder areas, and a starting point list for breeders. Mr. Wendel Levi of Sumpter, South Carolina took detailed notes on floral and foliar damage to his many camellia varieties after episodes of severe cold for many years. He published many reports as he obtained new information, and a final detailed summary appeared in 1973. His list of hardy cultivars was based on years of observation, and it was very reliable. It is still used as a basis for selecting camellias for gardens in the mid-Atlantic states of the United States.

In 1977 a particularly harsh winter did major damage to most cultivars in the camellia planting at the U.S. National Arboretum in Washington, DC, but *C. oleifera* sustained the least damage. Dr. William Ackerman noticed this survival and began a breeding program, initially with *C. sasanqua*, to develop hardier garden cultivars (Ackerman and Williams, 1981). This program has been highly successful and many cultivars of this parentage are being grown in the coldest areas where camellias can be cultivated. One of these cultivars, 'Twilight Glow', is pictured in Fig. 2.

Significant hardiness is found in species in cultivation in addition to *C. japonica*. The clones of *C. sasanqua* are nearly as hardy as *C. japonica*, but under the most severe cold stress, *C. japonica* is hardier; however, the difference in hardiness between the two species is not great. *C. cuspidata* and its few hybrids are approximately as hardy as *C. japonica*. The hybrids with *C. cuspidata* are very popular in England, for example *C. saluenensis* × *C. cuspidata* 'Cornish Snow'.

Hardiness has been observed in some clones of *C. sinensis*. Some of the shrubby forms with small leaves from Japan are as hardy as any *Camellia* accession we have tested, but the more arboreal forms from southern China with larger leaves are much less hardy. Despite the fact that the flowers of tea are less showy, the tea plant is a hardy and desirable evergreen for landscaping. There are many reports of tea being grown in colder areas of China, but never verified.

C. tenuivalvis was recently discovered on Longzhoushan Mountain near the town of Huili in southern Sichuan. For a picture of *C. tenuivalvis* see *Rhododendrons with Camellias and Magnolias 1999,* Fig. 6 on p.ii next to p.24. It is a diploid species closely related to *C. saluenensis*. It is abundant on the mountain up to a cleared meadow on a ridge at 3200m. It survives in the meadow as shrubs that have sprouted from stumps after deforestation. On the opposite side of the ridge, the mature *Lithocarpus* forest is intact, and *C. tenuivalvis* occurs there as a large shrub or small tree under the larger *Lithocarpus* trees. The flowers in this high elevation population are quite large and in shades of pink, and thus this species makes an excellent display in its natural habitat. It has been very difficult to establish in the eastern United States because it declines in humid, summer heat. We have been successful with several grafts. These flower, and we are able to make hybrids. It is easily hybridised with *C. japonica*.

C. saluenensis (*C. pitardii* var. *pitardii*) is widely distributed in Yunnan and Sichuan. It usually occurs as shrubs in dry, weedy, deforested fields, but a close examination often shows it to be regenerating from old stumps. Although it survives in dry open fields, it was originally a component of open woodlands. It flowers very freely and can make striking floral displays. It is readily crossed with *C. japonica* and these hybrids are known as *C.* × *williamsii*. These hybrids are important cultivars in most of the areas where camellias are cultivated. Some of these hybrids produce our best floral displays in gardens. *C. saluenensis* was recently identified as a small understory tree in the forests of Jizhushan (Chicken Foot Mountain near Dali, Yunnan). On that mountain it ranges up to nearly 3000m. The accessions of *C. saluenensis* from all localities do not tolerate the hot, humid summers of the eastern United States, and many of the *C.* × *williamsii* hybrids are also not at their best in these climates. Among these hybrids there is variation in resistance to fungal dieback diseases, and thus cultivars can be selected that are more tolerant of hot and humid climates.

A species recently obtained from hills south of the Yangtze River, *C. chekiangoleosa* (see Fig.4) is closely related to *C. japonica*. The flowers are larger and have more of an orange cast in the red pigmentation than the Japanese species. It hybridises readily with other species in Section *Camellia*. It has been out in test plots for a few years, and shown no cold injury symptoms so far; however, recent winters have been mild.

A species from Chekiang Province south of Shanghai is *C. octopetala* (see Fig. 6). It has cream to yellowish flowers in the autumn, and large leaves with impressed veins. It is distantly related to other camellias, and hybrids have not been successfully synthesised yet. It has been growing under garden conditions for several years, and it has survived temperatures down to -18°C (0°F) without apparent injury.

C. edithae is only known in cultivation as two double-flowered cultivars. One of these is a deep pink formal (see Fig.3) that flowers at the end of the flowering season in April. The leaves tend to be more cordate than other *Camellia* species and richly textured. It is an excellent garden plant, hardy at least to -18°C (0°F). This cultivar is male-sterile (all petals with no anthers), and it has not been possible to use in a crossing program. This is a striking *Camellia* variety with beautiful foliage and large, heat-resistant flowers that are produced after the weather has become warm.

We have recently obtained other species from western China that are ornamental and worthy of garden culture, but no information on them is yet available. Mr. Jimin Gao collected other high elevation forms from southwestern China, which might be sources of hardiness, but these also have not been established in cultivation outside of China.

Climate and Hardiness

Species native to climates with high summer temperatures may not readily adapt to cultivation in a climate with cool summer temperatures. *C. sasanqua* is native to southern Japan where summer temperatures are very high. In climates with cool summer weather such as England, many cultivars of *C. sasanqua* are poorly adapted and show delayed dormancy and reduced flower bud set. Since the cultivated forms of *C. sasanqua* mostly carry some genes from *C. japonica* (Parks *et al.*, 1981), it is likely that some cultivars will be better adapted to a climate with cool summers. Since *C. sasanqua* makes excellent floral dis-

plays in the autumn, it would be worth testing a large number of cultivars for adaptation to cool summer weather. Such a test should also include the hardy hybrids between *C. sasanqua* and *C. oleifera*, as well as the *C. × vernalis* hybrids (*C. sasanqua × C. japonica*).

While breeders of camellias might wish to develop a great cultivar that can be grown everywhere camellias are cultivated, it is better for the breeder to concentrate on selecting parents from a climate similar to the climate in which his cultivars will be grown. In most cases that means selecting the correct species since most species have their own unique adaptation. *C. japonica* provides a rare opportunity as it occurs naturally from northeastern Japan, an area with cool summers, to the Ryu Kyu Islands and Taiwan, areas with hot summers. For southern England, breeding stocks from northeastern Japan should be used, while for Sydney, Australia better results would come from Ryu Kyu accessions. When typical varieties of *C. japonica* are grown in a very mild climate such as south Florida, they refuse to set flower buds without minimal winter chilling. Because of great diversity in natural adaptation, we have the opportunity to breed *C. japonica* for both cool and hot climates. Breeding research is under way to improve cold hardiness, but investigators are only beginning to discuss breeding programs to develop warm-climate adaptations.

Other *Camellia* species exhibit various degrees of these problems. The *Camellia* species with yellow flowers are native to the hot climates of south central China and Vietnam. These set very few flower buds if grown in a climate with cool summers.

Experienced gardeners are aware of environmental factors that can modify hardiness. It has already been noted that species native to hot climates may not develop dormancy properly if grown in climates with cool summers. Drought conditions in the autumn will interfere with the development of dormancy. With respect to cooling in the autumn and winter, gradual cooling leads to a deeper dormancy (and less cold injury) than abrupt changes from warm to cold in the autumn. Sometimes it is possible to carefully select a site for a marginally hardy plant such as a *Camellia* in such a way that deeper dormancy will be achieved, and gardeners should pay close attention to site selection.

Levels of Hardiness

The hardiness level required for a given region needs to be carefully determined. Cultivars should be bred and selected for the climate extremes of the region in which they will be grown. In the following outline, *Camellia* hardiness is divided into three temperature zones. Germplasm that might be used to breed cultivars for each zone is listed. Different germplasm should be used to breed cultivars adequately hardy according to the severity of winter cold in each zone.

1. The coldest areas in which camellias can be cultivated (very infrequent events of -23°C/-10°F)
  a) *C oleifera* or its hybrids, particularly with *C. sasanqua*
  b) Hardiest selections of *C. japonica*
  c) Hardiest forms of tea
  d) High elevation species from western China

2. Moderately cold areas (very infrequent events of -18°C/0°F)
  a) Many moderately hardy species (*C. cuspidata, C. edithae, C. octopetala*, [see Fig. 6] etc.) and their hybrids
  b) Hardy segregants from combinations between tender species such as *C.*

reticulata and hardy species such as *C. japonica* or *C. sasanqua*.

3. Mild climates (very infrequent events of -8°C/18°F)
  a) Most species and hybrids

Breeding for Autumn Bloom

Breeding for cold resistance may be divided into broad categories according to the season of bloom. In colder regions there are three distinct advantages to having our bloom in the autumn:

1. There are few other shrubs blooming in the autumn season

2. The bloom season is finished by the onset of winter cold, and thus we do not need to be concerned with the hardiness of the flower buds. Only vegetative hardiness is essential.

3. In most of the regions where camellias are grown flowers are subject to flower blight infection in the spring; however, the causal fungus is not active before it is vernalised by winter cold. Fall infections do not occur.

The hardiness of the *C. sasanqua* × *C. oleifera* hybrids has already been mentioned. They tend to flower early in the autumn in the eastern United States and complete flowering before winter cold. These hybrids are easy to generate in large numbers, and thus it is relatively easy to identify a superior cultivar. They have become popular in the coldest area of the United States where camellias are cultivated, and they should be extensively tested in the parts of Western Europe where winter cold is a limiting factor in camellia cultivation.

Another group of hybrids that offer considerable hardiness and fall bloom is the highly variable hybrid group known as *C.* × *vernalis* (see Fig. 5). These are hybrids between *C. sasanqua* and *C. japonica* although most of them are more *C. sasanqua* than *C. japonica*. The flowering season is autumn, but often it is later than the *C. sasanqua* × *C. oleifera* hybrids. The *C.* × *vernalis* hybrids are popular in Japan, but only grown occasionally outside of Japan. Many cultivars are not only quite hardy, but also capable of outstanding floral displays. This group of hybrids should be explored by Western gardeners.

The hybrids between *C. sasanqua* and *C. reticulata* (see Fig. 7) are less hardy than pure *C. sasanqua*, and they bloom in early winter when the flowers may be damaged by the cold of early winter. The hybrid is very large and showy, but only suited for a milder climate. We backcrossed this hybrid to *C. sasanqua* to obtain good flowers on a hardier plant that bloomed earlier. Some of these backcrosses have produced excellent flowers and are relatively hardy and suitable for areas where temperatures do not go below -18°C (0°F).

Although we think of *C. japonica* as spring blooming, individuals vary greatly in their bloom time. Some varieties are known that flower in the autumn, and these are being tested for cold hardiness. There are now active breeding programs to select hardy, fall-blooming clones of *C. japonica*.

The tea plant blooms in autumn, and some selections are very hardy. These make excellent broadleaved evergreens in the garden. Hybrids with other species are generally difficult to synthesise.

Breeding for Spring Bloom

Our best possibility for the production of bloom in the spring is the hardy cultivars of *C. japonica*. There are many breeding and testing programs under way and several hardier cultivars have been introduced in recent years.

We have already discussed the potential for hardy hybrids using new camellias native to high elevations in western China. These breeding programs have barely begun, but it is too soon to predict what may be achieved by these endeavours.

Several hardy species such as *C. chekiangoleosa*, *C. cuspidata* and *C. edithae* can be readily hybridised with other species of *Camellia*. A few hybrids with *C. cuspidata* are widely cultivated and have good hardiness. *C. chekiangoleosa* and *C. edithae* hybridise readily with *C. japonica* and other related species. These hybrids are now established in field trials, and we should have information on hardiness as soon as these plants are exposed to severe winter cold.

Field Testing

As soon as seedlings bred for hardiness are germinated and established, they should be planted in field trials. After a few years exposed to the elements, it will become apparent which individuals are most tolerant of winter cold. In our area seedlings from the hardiest stocks of *C. japonica*, *C. sasanqua* × *C. oleifera* hybrids and some others are fully hardy most years. Our winter climate is not cold enough in most seasons to provide test winters. For these plants we propagate cuttings from each individual and send the rooted cuttings to Longwood Gardens in Pennsylvania for field testing.

While many plant breeders and nurseries maintain their private testing programs, there is not enough broad-spectrum testing being done on cultivars 'supposedly' cold resistant. Cultivar clones can react differently in different climates. A cultivar that has performed well in Maryland in the eastern United States may not perform as well in a climate with cool summers. New selections that have done well in preliminary tests should be planted with cultivars of known performance in several different localities. Such tests would allow us to rank cultivars and new introductions for their hardiness. Such information is only available in fragments from some test sites. There is a growing awareness of the need for more testing, and in the next few years more field performance information may be available.

Conclusions

Gardeners and nurserymen have made observations on the hardiness of *Camellia* cultivars since camellias became popular garden plants. It was found that varieties have different degrees of hardiness and the hardiness level is inherited. These observations became the basis for camellia breeding and development for the cooler areas where camellias are grown.

Since collectors had the opportunity to visit the areas in China where *Camellia* species occur naturally, many species have been introduced that may provide significant hardiness. Several of those species that seemed to have particular value were briefly discussed here.

The recently introduced species are just beginning to be included in breeding programs to develop hardier camellias. These programs should be pursued vigorously.

Because *Camellia* species are native to very different climates, they adjust differently to different climates in cultivation. For best performance in the garden, cultivars should be bred or selected for specific climatic patterns.

The testing phase of breeding camellias has been neglected. More emphasis should be placed on testing new selections and cultivars for hardiness performance.

References

ACKERMAN, W. L. and WILLIAMS, M. (1981). New Cold Hardy Camellia Hybrid Selections. *American Camellia Society Yearbook*: 117–120.

LEVI, W. (1973). Tenth Report on Varietal Differences in Cold Resistance of Camellia Buds. *American Camellia Society Yearbook*: 117–137.

PARKS, C. R., KONDO, K. and SWAIN, T. (1981). Phytochemical Evidence for the Genetic Contamination of *Camellia sasanqua*, Thunberg. *Japanese Journal of Breeding*, 31(2): 167–182.

Dr Clifford Parks is Professor in the Department of Biology at the University of North Carolina

The Revision of the RHS AGM List of Rhododendrons

John Hillier

The Award of Garden Merit was initiated in 1921 and after a somewhat chequered 50 years, of little focus and structure, was re-instituted in 1992, following a review of all plant awards within the Royal Horticultural Society.

The outcome of that review was to clarify the objectives of the various awards, namely that the Award of Garden Merit (AGM) would be for plants of outstanding excellence for garden decoration or use and would be subject to periodic review whereas the First Class Certificate (FCC), Award of Merit (AM) and Certificate of Preliminary Commendation (PC) would be for exhibition and would be permanent.

The AGM covers all ornamental plants, fruit and vegetables, whether hardy throughout the British Isles or requiring glass protection. In each case the purpose is to highlight the best plants available within the British Horticultural Trade. To achieve a reasonable standard across the wide range of plants, the plant committees were given the following directions:

The award may only be given after a period of assessment in one or more of the following:

1) Society trials or other trials run on similar lines
2) Visits to specialist collections
3) Round-table discussion drawing on the expertise and experience of the committee members and invited specialist if appropriate

The following criteria had to be taken into consideration during the assessment;

The plant should be:

a) excellent for ordinary garden decoration or use
b) of good constitution
c) available in the horticultural trade

The plant should not:

a) be particularly susceptible to any pest or disease
b) require highly specialised care
c) be subject to an unreasonable degree of reversion

The plant would also be subject to a hardiness rating as follows:

H1 = plants require heated glass
H2 = plants require unheated glass
H3 = plants hardy outside in some regions or in particular situations (microclimates) or that require frost-free protection
H4 = plants hardy throughout British Isles

At the February 2000 meeting of the Rhododendron and Camellia Committee, John Bond, as chairman, announced the start of a review process of the Award of Garden Merit. The process was to be completed by late summer 2001 for publication in spring

2002. To this end, the Chairman proposed that the current AGM list of Rhododendrons and Camellias be sent to each member of the committee with space for suggested deletions, additions and comments. Two sub-committees, one for Rhododendron the other for Camellia, would also be appointed to look at the findings during the summer of 2000 and report back to the full committee.

Discussion took place on what was meant by "available", the guideline suggested was that being used by Committee B namely that a plant should be listed in the *RHS Plant Finder* with at least two suppliers. However, it was felt that this did not fully reflect true availability for the ordinary gardener and that members should indicate if they knew otherwise.

At our early March 2000 meeting, discussion took place as to whether nurseries were selling certain rhododendron cultivars as Group or Award clones because the *RHS Plant Finder* had listed them as "Group and Clone" when nurseries had not made the distinction.

At our June 2000 meeting, chairman John Bond nominated the two sub-committees: for Camellias, Messrs Gallagher (chairman), Pharoah and Miss Trehane; for Rhododendrons, Messrs Hillier (chairman), Jack, Millais and Tomlin, both sub-committees to report back to the October meeting.

The Rhododendron sub-committee first met in late July 2000 to evaluate the responses from the main committee, together with recommendations from the woody plant trial of the relatively young *R. yakushimanum* hybrids. From the comments made across the 311 AGM plants we realised very early on that we had a difficult task ahead and made the following observations:

1) That many of the genus were of specialist interest only
2) That climate played a big part in what grew well where within the UK.
3) That species varied in some cases dramatically
4) That availability was limited, Rhododendrons having lost popularity over recent years with the consequence that there were few growers
5) The instability sometimes of micropropagated plants
6) The effect of pest and disease in recent years, particularly powdery mildew

At this point we wished we had a connoisseurs award! After a very full day we had deleted 59, added 38 and had many question marks, which we decided to take to the October meeting, for further guidance from the committee, and recommended we should invite input from Peter and Kenneth Cox, which subsequently took place.

At the committee meeting in October 2000, after long discussions on the problems raised by the sub-committee and other heart-searching questions about our beloved genus, it was agreed that the sub-committee had the additions about right, but that many more should be deleted.

The secretary was asked to produce a new voting form to include all suggestions of the sub-committee set out in four sections for clarity: 'species', 'hybrids', 'deciduous Azalea', and 'evergreen Azalea'. Four columns were also set out: 'yes to AGM', 'no to AGM', 'abstain', and 'comments'. Members were asked to return their voting papers by mid-January for the sub-committee to make a final recommendation to the March 2001 meeting.

By the committee's meeting in February 2001, the secretary was able to table the sub-committee recommendations and at the early March meeting, the sub-committee's recommendations were agreed. The final count being 136 deletions and 54 additions giving a total of 229 AGM Rhododendrons.

During the course of this review over 500 species and cultivars were considered in depth by the sub-committees. In addition to the plants awarded, a further list was compiled of a couple of dozen plants to keep an eye on for future consideration, but as yet do not qualify under the terms of reference. It is also expected further proposals are likely from the *R. yakushimanum* hybrid trials at Wisley, which still has a few years to run. All this is in line with the spirit of the AGM as new awards can be made prior to the next review.

I hope this account gives an insight into scale and thoroughness of the RHS Rhododendron and Camellia Committee's commitment to the RHS awards scheme. I should like to thank all those who spent many hours, both inside and outside committee times, in reaching the final conclusion.

The Camellia sub-committee's recommendations were to increase the AGMs from 82 to 94, being made up of 18 deletions and 32 additions.

The *AGM plants 2002* book is available from RHS shops, price £5.95.

John Hillier VMH is a member of the RHS Floral B Committee and also Chairman of the RHS Rhododendron and Camellia Committee

RHS AGM Review 2002: Rhododendron – Final List

R= suitable for a rock garden. (H4), etc = hardiness rating. d= double-flowered. Azalea classifications follow those in the *RHS Plant Finder*.

Rhododendron species and their cultivars (excluding azaleas)

argyrophyllum subsp. *nankingense* 'Chinese Silver' (H4)

augustinii 'Electra' (H3–4)

bureavii (H4)

calophytum (H4)

calostrotum 'Gigha' (H4) – suitable for small gardens; R

calostrotum subsp. *keleticum* (H4) – suitable for small gardens; R

campylogynum (H4) – suitable for small gardens; R

dauricum 'Midwinter' (H4)

davidsonianum (H3–4)

decorum (H4)

edgeworthii (H2–3)

falconeri (H3–4) – prefers light shade and shelter

fastigiatum 'Blue Steel' (H4) – suitable for small gardens; R

fortunei subsp. *discolor* (H4)

fulvum (H4)

hippophaeoides 'Haba Shan' (H4) – suitable for small gardens

insigne (H4)

keiskei var. *ozawae* 'Yaku Fairy' (H4) – suitable for small gardens; R

lutescens 'Bagshot Sands' (H3–4)

macabeanum (H3–4) – prefers light shade and shelter

makinoi (H4)

mucronulatum 'Cornell Pink' (H4)

niveum (H4)

orbiculare (H3–4)

oreodoxa var.fargesii (H4)

pachysanthum (H4)

polycladum (Scintillans Group) 'Policy' (H4) – i.e. the FCC clone of the Scintillans Group;

suitable for small gardens; R.
pseudochrysanthum (H4)

racemosum (H4) – suitable for small gardens

racemosum 'Rock Rose' ex R 11265 (H3–4) – suitable for small gardens

rex subsp. *fictolacteum* (H3–4) – prefers light shade and shelter

rex subsp. *rex* (H3–4) – prefers light shade and shelter

roxieanum var. *oreonastes* (H4) – suitable for small gardens

russatum (H4) – suitable for small gardens; R

sinogrande (H3) – prefers light shade and shelter

trichostomum 'Collingwood Ingram' (H4) – suitable for small gardens; R

williamsianum (H4) – suitable for small gardens

wiltonii (H4)

yakushimanum 'Koichiro Wada' (H4) – suitable for small gardens

yunnanense 'Openwood' (H3–4)

Rhododendron hybrid cultivars (excluding azaleas)

'Albert Schweitzer' (H4)

'Alice' (H4)

'Arctic Tern' – see *Ledodendron* (H4)

'Argosy' (H4) – prefers light shade and shelter

'Avalanche' (H4) – prefers light shade and shelter

'Bashful' (H4)

'Blewbury' (H4)

'Blue Peter' (H4)

'Bow Bells' (H4)

'Bruce Brechtbill' (H4) – suitable for small gardens

'Caroline Allbrook' (H4)

'Cetewayo' (H4)

'Champagne' (H3–4)

'Chevalier Felix de Sauvage' (H4)

'Choremia' (H3)

'Cilpinense' (H3–4) – suitable for small gardens; R

'Countess of Haddington' (H2)

'Crane' (H4) – suitable for small gardens

'Crest' (H3–4)

'Curlew' (H4) – suitable for small gardens; R

'Cynthia' (H4)

'David' (H4)

'Dopey' (H4) – suitable for small gardens

'Dora Amateis' (H4) – suitable for small gardens

'Dreamland' (H4) – suitable for small gardens

'Egret' (H4) – suitable for small gardens; R

'Elisabeth Hobbie' (H4) – suitable for small gardens

'Fabia' (H3)

'Faggetter's Favourite' (H4)

'Fantastica' (H4) – suitable for small gardens

'Fastuosum Flore Pleno' (d) (H4)

'Fragrantissimum' (H2–3)

'Frank Galsworthy' (H4)

'Furnivall's Daughter' (H4)

'Gartendirektor Rieger' (H4)

'Ginny Gee' (H4) – suitable for small gardens; R

'Golden Torch' (H4) – suitable for small gardens

'Goldkrone' (H4)

'Gomer Waterer' (H4)

'Gristede' (H4) – suitable for small gardens; R

'Hachmann's Marlis' (H4) – suitable for small gardens

'Hachmann's Polaris' (H4) – suitable for small gardens

'Helene Schiffner' (H4)

'Horizon Monarch' (H3–4)

'Hotei' (H4)

'Hydon Dawn' (H4) – suitable for small gardens

'Hydon Hunter' (H4)

'James Burchett' (H4)

'Kate Waterer' (H4)

'Kluis Sensation' (H4)

'Lady Alice Fitzwilliam' (H2–3)

'Lady Clementine Mitford' (H4)

'Lavender Girl' (H4)

'Lem's Cameo' (H3)

'Lem's Monarch' (H4)

'Linda' (H4) – suitable for small gardens

'Lodauric Iceberg' (H3–4) – prefers light shade and shelter

'Loderi Game Chick' (H3–4) – prefers light shade and shelter

'Loderi King George' (H3–4) – prefers light shade and shelter

'Loderi Pink Diamond' (H3–4) – prefers light shade and shelter

'Loderi Pink Topaz (H3–4) – prefers light shade and shelter

'Loderi Venus' (H3–4) – prefers light shade and shelter

'Loder's White' (H3–4)

'Lord Roberts' (H4)

'Marion Street' (H4) – suitable for small gardens

'Markeeta's Prize' (H4)

'May Day' (H3–4) – suitable for small gardens

'Merganser' (H4) – suitable for small gardens; R

'Moerheim' (H4) – suitable for small gardens; R

'Morning Cloud' (H4) – suitable for small gardens

'Mrs A.T. de la Mare' (H4)

'Mrs Charles E. Pearson' (H4)

'Mrs Davies Evans' (H4)

'Mrs Furnivall' (H4)

'Mrs J. C. Williams' (H4)

'Mrs Lionel de Rothschild' (H4)

'Mrs R.S. Holford' (H4)

'Mrs T.H. Lowinsky' (H4)

'Nancy Evans' (H3–4)

'Old Port' (H4)

'Olga' (H4)

'Osmar' (H4) – suitable for small gardens

'Patty Bee' (H4) – suitable for small gardens; R

'Penheale Blue' (H4) – suitable for small gardens

'Percy Wiseman' (H4) – suitable for small gardens

'Pink Cherub' (H4) – suitable for small gardens

'Pink Pebble' (H3–4) – suitable for small gardens

(PJM Group) 'Peter John Mezitt' (H4) – suitable for small gardens

'Polar Bear' (H3–4) – prefers light shade and shelter

'Praecox' (H4) – suitable for small gardens

'Princess Anne' (H4) – suitable for small gardens; R

'Professor Hugo de Vries' (H4)

'Ptarmigan' (H3–4) – suitable for small gardens; R

'Purple Splendour' (H4)

'Queen Elizabeth II' (H4)

'Ramapo' (H4) – suitable for small gardens; R

'Razorbill' (H4) – suitable for small gardens; R

'Rendezvous' (H4) – suitable for small gardens

'Renoir' (H4) – suitable for small gardens

'Saint Merryn' (H4) – suitable for small gardens; R

'Sarled' (H4) – suitable for small gardens; R

'Scarlet Wonder' (H4) – suitable for small gardens; R

'Sir Charles Lemon' (H3–4)

'Souvenir de Doctor S. Endtz' (H4)

'Souvenir of Anthony Waterer' (H4)

'Susan' (H4) – Williams's *R. campanulatum* hybrid

'Tatjana' (H4) – suitable for small gardens

'Taurus' (H4)

'Tessa Roza' (H4) – suitable for small gardens

'The Hon. Jean Marie de Montague' (H4)

'The Master' (H4)

'Tibet' (H3–4) – suitable for small gardens

'Tidbit' (H4) – suitable for small gardens

'Tortoiseshell Orange' (H3–4)

'Tortoiseshell Wonder' (H3–4)

'Unique' (H4) – Slocock's *R. campylocarpum* hybrid – suitable for small gardens (missed out of AGM book in error)

'Vanessa Pastel' (H3–4)

'Vintage Rosé' (H4) – suitable for small gardens

'Viscy' (H4)

'Vulcan' (H4)

'W.F.H.' (H4) – suitable for small gardens

'Wee Bee' (H4) – suitable for small gardens; R

'Winsome' (H3)

'Yellow Hammer' (H4)

Evergreen azaleas

'Addy Wery' (EA) (H3–4) – suitable for small gardens

'Alexander' (EA) (H4)

'Beethoven' (EA) (H3–4) – suitable for small gardens

'Blaauw's Pink' (EA) (H3–4) – suitable for small gardens

'Blue Danube' (EA) (H3–4) – suitable for small gardens

'Canzonetta' (EA) (H4) – suitable for small gardens

'Elsie Lee' (EA/d) (H3–4) – suitable for small gardens

'Florida' (EA/d) (H3–4) – suitable for small gardens

'Geisha Orange' (EA) (H4) – suitable for small gardens

'Hino-crimson (EA) (H3–4) – suitable for small gardens

'Hinomayo' (EA) (H3–4) – suitable for small gardens; R

'Irohayama' (EA) (H3–4) – suitable for small gardens

'Johanna' (EA) (H4) – suitable for small gardens

kiusianum (EA) (H4) – shows great variation but generally excellent; suitable for small gardens

'Mother's Day' (EA) (H4) – suitable for small gardens

nakaharae 'Mount Seven Star' (EA) (H4) – suitable for small gardens; R

'Niagara' (EA) (H3–4) – suitable for small gardens

'Orange Beauty' (EA) (H3–4) – suitable for small gardens

'Palestrina' (EA) (H3–4) – suitable for small gardens

'Panda' (EA) (H4) – suitable for small gardens

'Pink Pancake'(EA)(H4) – suitable for small gardens

'Purple Triumph' (EA) (H3)

'Purpurtraum' (EA) (H4) – suitable for small gardens

'Racoon' (EA) (H4) – suitable for small gardens

'Rosebud' (EA/d) (H3–4) – suitable for small gardens

'Squirrel' (EA) (H4) – suitable for small gardens

'Vuyk's Rosyred' (EA) (H4) – suitable for small gardens

'Vuyk's Scarlet' (EA) (H4) – suitable for small gardens

'Wombat' (EA) (H4) – suitable for small gardens

Deciduous azaleas

'Annabella' (K) (H4) – suitable for small gardens

'Berryrose' (K) (H4) – suitable for small gardens

'Bouquet de Flore' (G) (H4) – suitable for small gardens

'Cannon's Double' (K/d) (H4)

'Cecile' (K) (H4) – suitable for small gardens

'Coccineum Speciosum' (G) (H4) – suitable for small gardens

'Corneille' (G/d) (H4) – suitable for small gardens

'Daviesii' (G) (H4) – suitable for small gardens

'Doctor M. Oosthoek' (M) (H4) – suitable for small gardens

'Double Damask' (K/d) (H4) – suitable for small gardens

'Exquisitum' (O) (H4) – suitable for small gardens

'Fireball' (K) (H4) – suitable for small gardens

'Gibraltar' (K) (H4) – suitable for small gardens

'Homebush' (K/d) (H4) – suitable for small gardens

'Hotspur Red' (K) (H4) – suitable for small gardens

'Irene Koster' (0) (H4) – suitable for small gardens

'Klondyke' (K) (H4) – suitable for small gardens

luteum (A) (H4) – suitable for small gardens

'Martha Isaacson' (Ad) (H4) – suitable for small gardens

'Nancy Waterer' (G) (H4) – suitable for small gardens

'Narcissiflorum' (G/d) (H4) – suitable for small gardens

'Norma' (R/d) (H4) – suitable for small gardens

occidentale (A) (H4) – extremely varibale; suitable for small garden

'Persil' (K) (H4) – suitable for small gardens

'Pucella' (G) (H4) – suitable for small gardens

'Rosata' (Vs) (H4)

'Satan' (K) (H4) – suitable for small gardens

'Silver Slipper' (K) (H4) – suitable for small gardens

'Spek's Orange' (M) (H4) – suitable for small gardens

'Strawberry Ice' (K) (H4) – suitable for small gardens

'Summer Fragrance' (O) (H4) – suitable for small gardens

'Sunte Nectarine' (K) (H4) – suitable for small gardens

vaseyi (A) (H3–4) – suitable for small gardens

viscosum (A) (H4) – variable, but good in all forms; suitable for small gardens

'White Lights' (H4) – suitable for small gardens

'Whitethroat' (K/d) (H4) – suitable for small gardens

Rediscovering The Ghent Azaleas

Jim Inskip

The confidence of Victorian and Edwardian gardeners was supported by the availability of an enormous range of woody and herbaceous plants offered by the great 19th and early 20th Century nurseries and it was taken for granted that such a wide range would always be available. Never mind if our rare rhododendrons or azaleas should die, Veitchs would always have a replacement.

With the benefit of hindsight, we now know what a false assumption that was. Our generation has learned that "If you buy a home near a large nursery – you'll probably soon have a new housing estate next door," and that when we know that closure is imminent, we should acquire rarities before they are auctioned off as a job lot. Fortunately, some collections from the heyday have survived austerity and so many extremes of weather, providing a legacy of material for propagation of plants for the NCCPG. However, Ghent azaleas have not fared well in this respect, for, out of the 1,000 or more hybrids listed by former nurseries, we know only about 150 today.

New enthusiasts for these deciduous azaleas can be forgiven for assuming that all the named varieties have flowers that are small (commensurate with the predominance of eastern American species in their ancestry), because the rather scant azalea literature says so. This assumption is true for some of the early hybrids or variants of species of the 18th and 19th Centuries, such as those with latin names, but the gradual introduction of *R. luteum*, *R. molle* and *R. japonicum* into crosses meant that many later hybrids classified as Ghents had comparatively large flowers, for example 'Daviesii', 'Madame Moser', 'Nancy Waterer', 'Ada Bruniere' and 'Unique', and were not bred at Ghent at all. Some of those bred by Harry White at Sunningdale Nursery in the late 19th and early 20th Centuries had flowers of similar size, such as 'Mrs Harry White', 'Chieftain' and 'Crimson King'. John Waterer, Sons and Crisp introduced 'Orpheus' and 'Vulcan' in the same period.

Maybe size doesn't matter and in the words of Donald Waterer, "It has been a galling experience for many a modern breeder of azaleas, while showing off his most recent seedlings, to have observed his visitor's ecstasy at the sight of an elderly Ghent azalea in the background. Galling it may have been, but it has also been a reminder that the azalea that bears flowers 10–13cm (4–5in) in diameter may not necessarily outshine some of the azaleas our grandparents knew". 'Ghent' had become a generic term for all deciduous azalea hybrids (excluding Mollis hybrids) rather like Hoover and Biro, simply because the first well-known hybrids that entered the trade had been bred at Ghent. It was only from the 1930s onwards when new hybrids, introduced by Knap Hill and Exbury began to be known as Knap Hill azaleas ('the Knap Hill strain'), that John Waterer, Sons and Crisp called their introductions 'New Ghent' hybrids.

Another misconception about Ghent azaleas is that they are all late flowering, suggesting that they flower after the Mollis, Knap Hill and Exbury hybrids. This came about because when Mollis hybrids were introduced in the late 19th and early 20th Centuries, their flowering period was a fortnight or more earlier than that of most Ghent azaleas, although some of these, such as 'Crocea Tricolor', 'Nosegay' and 'Decorator' bloomed alongside the mainstream Mollis plants. 'Phidias' is one of the earliest flowering of all deciduous azaleas. Yet today we see most Ghents blooming at the same time as the main Knap Hill and Exbury season, and the very late hybrids bloom at the same time as the very late season Knap Hill hybrids – this is to be expected because the late-flowering character of both groups has been inherited from American native species such as *R. calendulaceum*, *R. cumberlandense* and *R. viscosum*, mostly by years of hybridisation but occasionally by direct back crosses with such species. Not all Ghent azaleas are fragrant, just as not all later hybrids are fragrant, and the same is true for autumnal leaf colours.

To find Ghent azaleas other than, say, 'Coccineum Speciosum' and 'Narcissiflorum', is perhaps more difficult than finding other groups of plants because so many were

introduced so long ago and have died through neglect or clearance to make way for a 'new' garden. If nurtured, azaleas will live for many years – 100 or more. The original plant of 'Viscosepala' (*viscosum* × *molle*), raised before 1842, still grows at Knap Hill Nursery. The major nurseries that specialised in these azaleas closed many years ago and it is a rare delight to find a garden with a surviving collection, backed up with original planting plans, labels or lists of plants purchased. It is worth noting that Gertrude Jekyll used 'Daviesii' and other Ghent azaleas extensively at her home Munstead Wood in Surrey and at Walsham House in Elstead.

A further difficulty is that there are very few pictorial portraits, usually chroma-lithographs, leaving us to rely on descriptions in various nursery catalogues, which quite often differed although describing the same plant or, even worse, the same name had been given to different plants. As a criterion for deciding which must be a true plant with its correct name, we should surely accept the name and descriptions provided by the majority of nurseries whence most of the Ghent azaleas originated, including Van Houtte and the Verschaffelts in Belgium, the Rinz brothers in Frankfurt, Germany and Moser at Versailles. Most of their descriptions can be matched to those in Veitch's catalogues and in *Rhododendrons and their various Hybrids* by J.G. Millais, published in 1917 and 1924.

Changed descriptions crept in gradually during the 1920s onwards, but because so many varieties appeared so similar, confusion was not surprising, particularly among the 'Rustica Flore Pleno' and double-flowered Ghent plants. In the late 19th Century,

'Norma' was described as having flesh-coloured flowers, shaded with pale pink and having slightly crimped edges (catalogues of Van Houtte and Vuylsteke). Somehow 'Norma' became bright rose and rosy red (J.Waterer, Sons and Crisp; G. Reuthe) and this is presumably the salmon-rose flower we see today. 'Freya' was originally mauve-white and a tender lilac towards the edges. The base of the petals was yellow and gold – a perfect double (Van Houtte and Vuylsteke). The 'Freya' we see today is the one described in the International Rhododendron Register (IRR) 1958 – nankeen, tinted salmon-orange.

'Byron' was described by Van Houtte, Vuylsteke and Millais as having pure white, crimped, rounded, and undulated petals. The 'Byron' of today is white, tinged red. An obvious, intriguing question is whatever happened to the 'Freya' and 'Byron' of the original descriptions? And if the modern versions are impostors, what are their real identities?

Van Houtte, Vuylsteke, Van Geert and Veitch described 'Bartholo Lazzari' as having flesh pink flowers but from the 1930s this hybrid has been described as having orange-yellow buds, opening to orange-yellow flowers, fading to yellow, and this is the plant we see in modern collections.

'Bijou de Gentbrugge' was available from the old Belgian nurseries and from Veitch as a very double white flower, edged rose. Sunningdale was the only nursery to advertise 'Bijou de *Gandbruges*' as having flowers and anthers of rich, flame pink – this must have been a different plant. Among the single-flowered varieties, 'Josephine Klinger' was described as having crimson flowers with whitish spots. The International Rho-dodendron Register of 1958 described the flowers as salmon-pink with a yellow blotch. Two forms of 'Fama' were distributed: that of Van Houtte, Vuylsteke and others was violet and crimson, but Sunningdale offered plants with salmon and sulphur flowers. 'Aurore de Royghem' (Rooighem is a suburb of Ghent) was described, as the name suggests, as having flowers of yellow, shaded orange, the upper petal of a deeper yellow. Sunningdale nursery grew a plant with this name but their version had flowers of pale rose with a soft yellow top petal. Sunningdale's 'Vulcan' had flowers of Chinese yellow, flushed carmine-red, but Waterer's 'Vulcan', a later introduction mentioned above, had blood red flowers – both 'Vulcans' exist today. Some hybrids appear to have been given two names, for example 'Roi des Belges' was also called 'Mme Gustave Guilmot'; 'Dr (Directeur) Charles Baumann' was also known as 'Anna Louise'; and 'Beaute Celeste' had the alternative name of 'Cardinal'. Most books describe the fairly common, deep strawberry rose flowered plant known as 'Pucella' as having the alternative name of 'Fanny', but the true plant of 'Fanny' had flowers of nankeen yellow, spotted orange in the throat (Van Houtte et al). Listed in "Wilson and Rehder" 1921 we find Eugenie, Lemaire in *Ill. Hort.* II pl.75, fig.6 (1855) and Eugenie, Ottolander, *Neder. Fl. Pom.* 51, t.15, fig.3 (1876), not the same as the preceding variety.

Despite the difficulties discussed above, many 'lost' Ghent hybrids have been identified, photographed, rescued and propagated during the last five or six years. Albert de Raedt (author of an excellent book on these plants – *De Harde Gentse*), Leon Declercq and Jozef Delvaux have discovered many in

Belgian and German arboreta. Malcolm Nash and I have found several hybrids in Britain, such as the beautiful 'Van Houtte Flore Pleno' (see Fig.11), 'Bijou de Gentbrugge' (see Fig.13), 'Pontica Chromatella' (see Fig.10) (a pink semi-double, not the better known double yellow flowered plant, 'Chromatella'), 'Roi des Feux', 'Fidele Mechelynck', 'Alice Waterer', 'Sinensis Rosea', 'Nosegay', 'Ariel' and possibly 'Standishii' (see Fig.12) (this would be very important because of the Standish & Noble connection).

In our collection we now have the following Ghent and RFP Azaleas:

'Ada Bruniere', 'Admiraal de Ruyter', 'Aida', 'Alba Grandiflora', 'Alice Waterer', 'Altaclerense', 'Altaclerense Sunbeam', 'Anna Louise'/ 'Directeur Charles Baumann', 'Apelles', 'Ariadne', 'Ariel', 'Aurore de Royghem', 'Bartholo Lazzari', 'Beaute Celeste', 'Beaute de Flandre', 'Belle Merveille', 'Bijou de Gentbrugge', 'Bijou des Amateurs', 'Blood Red', 'Bouquet de Flore', 'Bronze Unique', 'Charlemagne', 'Chromatella', 'Clotilde', 'Coccinea Major', 'Coccineum Speciosum', 'Comte de Flandre', 'Comte d'Egmont', 'Corneille', 'Crocea Tricolor', 'Cuprea Aurantia', 'Cuprea Pulchella', 'Cymodocee', 'Daviesii', 'Delicata', 'Domenico Scassi', 'Durante Alle', 'Electra', 'Emile', 'Emma', 'Eugenie', 'Fama', 'Fenelon', 'Fidele Mechelynck', 'Flameola Incarnata', 'Francois de Taye', 'Frederick de Merode', 'Freya', 'Fritz Quihou', 'General Trauff', 'Gloria Mundi', 'Goldlack', 'Graf Alfred von Niepperg', 'Graf von Meran', 'Grandeur Triomphante', 'Guelder Rose', 'Guillaume II', 'Heroine', 'Heureuse Surprise', 'Hollandia', 'Honneur de Flandre', 'Hora', 'Igneum Novum', 'Il Tasso', 'Joseph Baumann', 'Josephine Klinger', 'Julda Schipp', 'Juliana Nova', 'Julius Caesar', 'La Surprise', 'Laelia', 'Leibuir', 'Lelie', 'L'Esperance', 'Louis Hellebuyck', 'Louis Aime Van Houtte', 'Madame Moser', 'Maja', 'Marie Verschaffelt', 'Mathilde', 'Mecene', 'Milton', 'Mina Van Houtte', 'Minerva', 'Miniata Floribunda', 'Mme Gustave Guilmot'/'Roi des Belges', 'Moorgold', 'Mrs Harry White', 'Murillo', 'Nancy Waterer', 'Narcissiflorum', 'Nero', 'Nivalis Striata', 'Norma', 'Nosegay', 'Orpheus', 'Oscar 1', 'Pallas', 'Phoebe', 'Phidias', 'Praxiteles', 'Prince Henri de Pays Bas', 'Princesse Charlotte', 'Proteus', 'Pucella', 'Quadricolor', 'Queen of England', 'Queen Victoria', 'Quentin Metsys', 'Racine', 'Raphael de Smet', 'Reine des Rouges', 'Ribera', 'Richardissima', 'Roi des Feux', 'Rose de Flandre', 'Rose Marie', 'Rouge Brique', 'Rubra Splendissima', 'Sang de Gentbrugge', 'Semiramis', 'Sessostris', 'Sinensis Rosea', 'Souvenir du President Carnot', 'Splendens', 'Standishii ?', 'Sully', 'Teniers', 'Thisbe', 'Unique', 'Van Houtte Flore Pleno', 'Variegata', 'Velazquez', 'Versicolor', 'Virgil', 'Vulcan' (Red), 'Wilhelmine' and 'Willem III'.

Some of the newly discovered and propagated plants (on their own roots) have been added to the National Collection that was founded with plants sent from Sunningdale Nursery via Castle Howard by the late Jim Russell to Sheffield Park.

At this point, it is worth warning any reader who has old, overgrown or unruly azaleas, possibly Ghents, not to prune them hard until the following steps have been taken, because if they were grafted plants with *R. luteum* rootstock, the *luteum* could take over and kill whatever of the grafted hybrid remained. First, if you notice that some stems of your old plant have largish, very fragrant yellow flowers and the rest have flowers of what the hybrid should be, the yellow-flowered stems should be removed at ground level whilst still in flower, before the rogue stems become less-easily recognised. Once it has been found that all the overgrown stems are those of the genuine hybrid, it would be wise to prune one-third of the shrub down to about 9in just as the buds are breaking in the following spring and the other two-thirds next two years. Complete hard pruning all at once can result in failure to regenerate.

Exhaustive studies of old catalogues and discoveries of plants now make it possible to amend the International Rhododendron Register with information that was not available to the compiler in 1958. Similarly, some of the descriptions in *Azaleas* by the late Fred Galle (Timber Press) require revision, since they were substantially based on IRR descriptions.

If several old collections have been found to contain what appears to be the same hybrid, albeit unidentified at present, it has been propagated in the hope of future identification. If you know of any Ghent Azaleas in gardens that you think that we are unaware of, please contact the author before it is too late!

References

AMERICAN HORTICULTURAL SOCIETY, The (1952) *The Azalea Handbook.*

BOWERS, Clement Gray (1954). *Winter Hardy Azaleas and Rhododendrons.*

BOWERS, Clement Gray (1960). *Rhododendrons and Azaleas.*

DAVIS, Nigel (1999). Hardy Ghent Azalea National Collection, *Rhododendrons with Camellias and Magnolias 1999.* Royal Horticultural Society.

DE KERCHOVE, Count Renaud (1995). Deciduous Azaleas: The Hybrids, *The Rhododendron Story.* Royal Horticultural Society.

DE RAEDT, Albert (1998). Hardy Ghent Azaleas, *Rhododendrons with Camellias and Magnolias 1998.* Royal Horticultural Society.

DE RAEDT, Albert (2000). *De Harde Gentse.*

FRASER, H. *Ornamental Conifers, Rhododendrons and other American Shrubs.*

GALLE, Fred C. (1987). *Azaleas* (Revised Edition).

GROOTENDORST, Herman J. (1954). *Rhododendrons and Azaleas.*

HAWORTH-BOOTH, Michael (1961). *The Flowering Shrub Garden.*

HUME, H. Harold (1948). *Azaleas: Kinds and Culture.*

JOHNSON, A.T. (1948). *Rhododendrons, Azaleas, Magnolias, Camellias, & Ornamental Cherries.*

LEE, Frederic (1959). *The Azalea Book.*

MILLAIS, J.G. (1917/1924). *Rhododendrons and their various Hybrids.*

RAND JR, E. S. (1871). *The Rhododendron and American Plants.*

RUSSELL, James (1960). *Rhododendrons at Sunningdale.*

SKINNER, Archie (1983). Rescuing Ghent Azaleas, *The Garden.* Royal Horticultural Society.

STREET, Frederick (1959). *Azaleas.*

WATERER, G. Donald (1958). Ghent Azaleas, *Rhododendron Yearbook 1958.* Royal Horticultural Society.

WILSON & REHDER (1921). *A Monograph of Azaleas.*

Jim Inskip is a member of the Wessex Branch of the Group and has a private nursery

Rhododendrons in Australia and New Zealand

Peter Cox

When we received invitations late in 1997 to give some lectures in New Zealand and later Australia for September to November 2000, my wife and I thought that at the age of over 65, and supposedly semi-retired, we would make a decent trip of it and spend three weeks in each country. Neither of us had been to either country before.

A night-and-day stopover in Singapore of course included the famous Botanic Gardens and we were not disappointed. The collection of palms is quite outstanding and the orchids are very fine but mostly hybrids, surely not appropriate for a botanic garden. We arrived in Sydney when the Olympic Games were still going and made our way directly to Tasmania, which had long been on our list of 'must go to' places.

Tasmania must have one of the best climates in the world for growing a huge range of plants. It might be thought that lying off the southern tip of mainland Australia and with plants with the specific epithet of antarctica that it might be a cold place, but coastal parts are virtually frost free. In the mountainous interior, it is a different story. Wind can be severe as we experienced on the top of Mt. Wellington behind Hobart where we reckoned its strength more than we had ever met anywhere else. South and central Tasmania have a thin soil, sandy and acid with some clay and black peat with rocks near the surface. In contrast, the north has some deep red soil. One decided disadvantage in having such favourable conditions is that introduced plants, pests and diseases also flourish. Rhododendron powdery mildew and rust had only appeared quite recently but looked like being devastating in their severity as does petal blight. Later we found that mainland Australia also suffers from serious diseases and pests of rhododendrons with thrips and lacebug seriously disfiguring foliage.

We spent part of our time visiting gardens and nurseries, the rest out in the wild looking for native plants. We stayed with Ken and Lesley Gillanders who have a most interesting nursery near Hobart, and Ken is an authority on the native flora, some of which he took us to see. Our timing for the gardens was perfect but we were too early for most of the local flora, such as most members of the family Epacridaceae, which is closely related to Ericaceae. *Richea* is a spectacular genus in Tasmania and most are endemic. The gardens varied from very steep hillsides to nicely landscaped slopes, and we were often very impressed with what we saw. One garden belonging to Barry and Lorraine Davidson on the coast had a flourishing collection of Vireya rhododendrons in the open ground by the house and then a bank down to a stream with some fine magnolias including *M.* 'Apollo' and *M.* 'Star Wars', the latter being one of the best for Tasmania with weather-resistant flowers produced over a long period. We saw some rhododendrons that have either died out in cultivation in the UK or are not satisfactory in our climate, including the fine tender yellow *R. boothii* (*mishmiense*) and the southern Chinese *R. mariesii* with attractive rose-coloured flowers. In Tasmania, Victoria and much of New Zealand, the tender (for us) Maddenia rhododendrons and their hybrids can be considered the ideal plants for their conditions and are vigorous and extremely easy to grow. Several hybrids in this group have been raised out there and we particularly liked *R.* 'Anne Teese' (*R. ciliicalyx* × *R. formosum* var. *formosum*).

Any thoughts that I would get fed up with the sight of endless eucalyptus were soon banished and I even collected some seed for attempting to grow more at Glendoick and Baravalla. Massive *E. regnans* rival the redwoods of California for size. There were no flowers yet on the prickly, multi-coloured *Richea scoparia* at Mt Field National Park and fresh slushy snow soon drove us off the mountain. That evening a half-tame wombat bit my ankle while we were eating our dinner. They are much larger and heftier than I expected.

On the north coast of Tasmania is the comparatively new Emu Gardens where again vireyas can be grown outside. I was surprised to find so few plants from the masses of newly collected and re-collected Rhododendron species from China etc., and very few species true to name. The big-leaved species had obviously been grown from open-pollinated seed, with *R. magnificum* and *R. macabeanum* about the only ones

true to name. Choniastrum species do well here and there were good *R. latoucheae* and *R. stamineum*. Unfortunately much of this potentially fine garden has little or no shade and the plants are suffering accordingly.

Arriving in Victoria, the garden of the Australian Rhododendron Society at Olinda in the Dandenongs was quite an eye opener. About 100 acres, this garden, like the Emu one, is largely maintained by volunteers. With such a large area and only two hours to spare there, we divided into groups. We (surprise, surprise) chose the species (so called) and like Emu, the majority had been grown from open-pollinated seed and among the big-leaved plants, only *R. protistum* was true to type (Graham Smith of Pukeiti fully agreed with me on the lack of real species). There were some fine *R. arboreum* in a good variety of forms, and it was interesting to see several plants of the rare Glischra, *R. vesiculiferum*.

The favourable ecological conditions in both southeast Australia and New Zealand have led to many introduced animals, birds and plants flourishing and frequently becoming pests. Many of our European birds were introduced and these are often doing much better there than they are now doing at home, for instance sparrows, starlings and thrushes. Alien plants are so liable to run amok that the governments only allow in seeds of plants that are familiar to them. Our native broom and gorse are among the worst introductions. We even saw embothriums and cardiocrinums happily naturalising. Opossums were introduced from Australia into New Zealand and these are a major pest for damaging trees and shrubs.

Our stay in New Zealand started with Dunedin where Brent Murdoch has done much to introduce many of the newly collected species into cultivation there, being first rate at raising them from seed. Brent and Graham Smith of Pukeiti are largely responsible for distributing and establishing plants from many of the recent expeditions to south-east Asia.

Dunedin Botanic Garden is well worth a visit. We were surprised to find that it cannot be closed to the public and one day we were there was a public holiday; there was no staff around, and yet pilfering plants does not seem to be a problem. Most rhododendrons were doing well but the dwarfs in peat beds were struggling. At one time there had obviously been little other than old 'hardy' hybrids and azaleas planted and there are still too many rather tired old hybrids. These could be gradually removed (so as not to cause a public outcry by scrapping too many in one go) and replaced by species, especially big-leaved ones in the well-sheltered area around the board walks. I observed that the American hybrid *R.* 'Else Frye' is not the same clone that we grow in Scotland and my subsequent trip to the Pacific Northwest of the USA proved that there are two clones of this fine hybrid (probably a cross of *R. ciliicalyx* × *R. edgeworthii*).

I noted two New Zealand hybrids at the local Dunedin show. *R.* 'Lalique' has large conical trusses of frilled, white-tinged pink and lilac flowers. *R.* 'Golden Dream' (*R. macabeanum* × *R. griffithianum*) had the largest flowers in the largest truss I think I have ever seen but unlike some other large-flowered hybrids, this one has quality.

We visited several gardens around and out of Dunedin. We were particularly impressed with the Fitchett's garden and Larnach Castle. It was nice to see large plants of the true *R. burmanicum*. What is usually called *R. burmanicum* in Britain is undoubtedly *R. burmanicum* × *R. valentinianum*. The rich yellow, newly introduced *R. valentinianum* var. *oblongilobatum*, which is very different from the type with much larger leaves and much later flowers, had recently been planted out, as had the rare *R. vialii*, which has striking red flowers. Some vireyas are difficult to grow on their own roots including the beautiful *R. himantodes*. In one garden this had been grafted on to the commonest and most easily grown vireya species, *R. macgregoriae*, with excellent results.

We were determined not to spend our whole time looking at gardens and to get out into the country to see the native flora and scenery. Our old friends Peter and Margaret Cameron organised a wonderful tour for us but sadly were unable to go with us owing to a nasty accident Margaret had had in Canada. Highlights were our visit to the Borland Saddle near Lake Manapouri with Professor Alan Mark, a great authority on New Zealand plants, and by ourselves to Mt Cook, on a beautiful day, with many of the glorious white *Ranunculus lyallii* in flower. We also made a short visit to the west coast with its soggy rainforest.

Outside Christchurch on the Canterbury Plain we stayed with our long-time friends Ted and Louise Somers. Their fine mature garden has one of the best rhododendron collections in New Zealand. It was nice to see rare species like *R. collectianum* and *R. viscidifolium* plus large specimens of several of my own dwarf hybrids such as *R.* 'Ptarmigan', *R.* 'Chikor' and *R.* 'Curlew'. Like elsewhere, it was noticeable that it was not a great flowering season. Canterbury Plain is a very flat area and can have light spring frosts, including one a few weeks before our visit, and also suffers from flooding.

Their lowest winter temperature is about -50°C. As in other parts of New Zealand and Australia, the growth there is much faster than we get in Scotland, especially of trees. I was impressed with the success of tall pine hedges used for shelter on the plain, which much to my surprise stand up well to pruning.

It was now time to move on to the North Island and to visit and to give a talk at Pukeiti Garden. Graham Smith, who has been director for many years, gave us a tremendous tour of this great garden, spread off and on over three days. It is undoubtedly one of the finest gardens in the world and run with a minimum of staff. The winters are just too cold for successful cultivation of vireyas outside, but with unheated protection they are grown to perfection. I was surprised at the number of cool-temperate *Rhododendron* species that do well, such as the Taiwanese species *R. pachysanthum* and *R. morii*. The one original plant of *R. protistum* from Kingdon Ward's 1954 expedition is several times bigger than those of the same vintage in Britain. With the 140-inch rainfall, growth is tremendous, but the near-ideal conditions for so many plants means that they may keep growing at the expense of starting to flower. As would be expected, species of Section *Choniastrum* (formerly Stamineum Series) do well but usually take many years to flower. Graham intends to try them in full sun to see if they well perform quicker. Quite a number of species have yet to be tried at Pukeiti and the severe restrictions on importing plants and seeds makes it difficult to bring things in.

Our last-but-one New Zealand visit was to Jeremy Thomson's farm where our friend Sashel Dayal also lives. The farm lies a little to the north of Pukeiti and it is not quite so wet. These two have done collecting in China and parts of India and Burma (Myanmar), which are normally very difficult to get into. Among their collections are new introductions of *R. macabeanum* and *R. elliottii* from the Naga Hills and *R. sinofalconeri* from southeast Yunnan. Jeremy is a pioneer at forestry farming and has many carefully tended plantations on his amazingly undulating terrain. Parts of these plantations have been planted up with numerous seedlings of these *Rhododendron* species and once the trees give a bit more protection, they should flourish. This introduction of *R. macabeanum* is a little different foliage-wise to the old introductions and is exceedingly vigorous. They are not old enough to start flowering.

Jeremy and Sashel took us to the famous Jury garden where so many good rhododendron, magnolia and camellia selections have originated. Mark Jury showed us many of his new crosses including hybrids between all the species of *Michelia* in cultivation. Some of these should make superb introductions for really mild gardens with masses of white scented flowers. Mark pointed out that even with michelias, scent can be elusive, with some crosses that should be scented, having none. There were huge specimens of *Michelia doltsopa* and *Magnolia nitida* the latter with its intensely dark shiny evergreen leaves. The brightly coloured Jury *R. cinnabarinum* × *R. maddenii* crosses were very fine, especially *R.* 'Bernice'.

We drove across to the drier east side of the North Island to the Hudsons at Gwavas where the rainfall is 40–50in. Michael and Carola are the parents of Tom Hudson who inherited the garden of Tregrehan in Cornwall. Gwavas has a really great collection of trees and shrubs and it was noticeable that the rhododendrons here were healthier than anywhere we had been. This may be partly due to less problems from diseases in this drier climate, but I have been gradually developing an opinion that rhododendrons really grow better and live longer in areas with moderate rainfall as opposed a heavy rainfall, provided that they are not over stressed by drought and drying winds during the growing season and that the soil is really suitable. Both in Britain and the Pacific Northwest of North America, I keep on being astounded by the quality of foliage and health in young to old age of plants in lower rainfall areas, while those in apparently ideal conditions with heavy rainfall may either have poor foliage or be comparatively short lived.

Mike Hudson has made several hybrids among the larger members of subsection Maddenia in the Dalhousiae Alliance and *R. megacalyx*. While very fine, I did not think that any were improvements on their parents. This was another fine rhododendron collection with many new introductions from Tom's collections in Vietnam and Yunnan.

Our journey home was via Bangkok where again we spent a night and a day, definitely to be recommended for breaking such a long journey. We had really enjoyed our first trip 'down under' and hope to return before too long.

Peter Cox VMH is a member of the Group, the author of several standard works on rhododendrons and has made many plant hunting trips to China, the Himalayas and elsewhere . He is a Director of Glendoick Gardens Ltd, Perth

MAGNOLIA STELLATA – THE SPECIES AND THE CULTIVARS

MIKE ROBINSON

The widespread flowering of the magnolias in suburban gardens is one of the first signs that winter is on the wane. I can become just a bit blasé about 'just another *M. soulangeana*', but I never feel that when confronted by a shrub of *M. stellata*. Not only are the flowers very beautiful, but the plant seems to enjoy all aspects, not require coddling, and has an attractive and shrubby habit of growth. Add to this that it tolerates pruning, it fits into a small space, is wind tolerant, and that its flowers are frost resistant, and you can understand why it is really popular.

Other than the 'common' white *M. stellata* with 12–14 tepals, there are at the time of writing, 28 different varieties of *M. stellata* listed in the TMS checklist of cultivars[1], of which 16 are listed by Wim Rutten[2], 17 by Eisenhut[3], and ten are listed as currently available to UK growers in the *RHS Plant Finder*[4]. The purpose or this article is to examine why such a wide range of varieties continue to be available, to say something about their origin and their value to gardeners today, and briefly to consider the newer hybrids.

Ignoring taxonomy for the moment, the first thing must be to ask what one generally expects from *stellata* magnolias in the garden:

- Attractive, scented, star-shaped flowers with least twelve tepals giving a semi-double or double effect.

- Compact growth – wider than high – at best a tiered effect.
- Some resistance to frost when in flower.
- Varieties with pink flowers, the depth of colour varying with climate and how far the flowers are open (q.v.).

The Species

While there has never been any doubt that our magnolia comes from Japan and was introduced to the USA by a Dr Hall in 1861 and to Russia by Maximowicz in 1872, its taxonomic history has been confused and complicated until very recently. The species is known as Shidekobushi in Japan. Unfortunately this has been translated differently by two authorities: the first is '*kobus* of homes' and is related to the fact that many Japanese have grown *M. stellata* inside as a pot plant, but the second is given as 'zig-zag petaled *kobus*' – both seeming to regard the plant as a variety of *M. kobus*.

The American introduction was named *M. halleana*, and the Russian one *M. stellata*. Fortunately for everyone but Dr Hall and his descendants, the name *stellata* had already been used to describe the plant in 1846 when the name *Buergeria stellata* was assigned to the type species by Siebold and Zuccarini. *Buergeria* later being recognised as a section of *Magnolia*. The name *tomen-*

tosa has also been used and rejected, so *M. stellata* it is, and quite right too!

What is also clear from the literature is that the early introductions were of cultivars from Japanese nurseries, not from the wild, and it became accepted by some authorities that *M. stellata* did not exist in the wild but was the result of continued selection and breeding in Japan over the centuries of extreme forms of *M. kobus*. As late as 1952 Blackburn[5], quoting Matsumara, the director of Nikko Botanic Garden, stated 'Japanese botanists do not consider *M. stellata* indigenous to their country, even though it is now encountered in the wild in southern Japan'. In other words in the wild it was merely an escapee from nurseries. One of the results of this was that *M. stellata* was classified as a variety of *M. kobus* by Callaway[6], following Spongberg and others. Furthermore, there was some doubt about *M. stellata* breeding true from seed at this time, but it has since been shown to do so.

More recent work, however, has identified a stable and isolated wild population in Japan, and it is now accepted that *M. stellata* is a species in its own right. Spongberg[7] gives a good summary of reasons for this, and his Fig.7 gives a very useful indication of the morphological differences between *M. kobus*, *M. salicifolia* and *M. stellata*. Ohba[8], the Japanese Association of Shidekobushi Conservation[9], and Gardiner[10] extend and reinforce the species nature of *M. stellata* from work on the wild population.

This wild population is quoted as limited to an area about 100km in diameter near the Southeast coast of central Honshu – for a map see Ohba[8]. It occurs at low altitude and is 'always found in sunny positions with a slight water flow'. This particular part of

Japan is unusual botanically, being characterised by the occurrence of many semi-endemic and endemic species, *Acer pycnanthum* being a good example[11]. It is important to note that *M. kobus*, widespread throughout Japan, does not occur in this area, but *M. salicifolia* does, and that while natural hybrids of *M. stellata* with *M. kobus* do not, of course, occur, hybrids with *M. stellata* (*M. × proctoriana*) have been reported[9,10]. These hybrids have the green leaf underside of *M. stellata*, not the glaucous colour of *M. salicifolia*, so it is not impossible such hybrids have been confused with *M. stellata*. Still more important is the variety within the wild stands: flowers vary in size from 5–12.5cm (2–5in) across, in colour from pure white to deep pink, and in tepal number from 12–40. The habit is usually shrubby and generally does not exceed 3m (10ft), although it can reach 6m (20ft). On drier slopes, however, it grows as a tree and may reach 7m (22ft).

M. stellata is thus safely established as a species with a distinct morphology, breeding true from seed but with a wide range of flower sizes, colours, tepal numbers and habits in the wild as well as in cultivation. It has more tepals because some of the stamens have become petaloid; the more tepals the fewer stamens. It is easily distinguishable from *M. kobus* which has a tree-like habit and normally 6(–9) tepals, but the distinction between taxa of *M. stellata* and *M. × loebneri* may not be quite so clear. The name *loebneri* should only be attached to hybrids between *M. stellata* and *M. kobus*, but whether this rule has been rigidly applied needs further research, particularly as tree-like *M. stellata* specimens have been found in the wild. *M. × proctoriana* hybrids from Japan possibly labelled *M. stellata* may have been circulating in Japan and the West independently of the hybridisation occurring in the USA from 1928 onwards[12]. Thus it is likely that most plants from Japanese nurseries are selections straight from the wild populations of *M. stellata* or breeding from these. What remains uncertain is whether any hybrids with *M. salicifolia* have been distributed as *M. stellata*, and if any *M. × loebneri* specimens are being so distributed. The change of growth habits induced by the common Japanese practice of grafting *M. stellata* on to *M. kobus* needs careful research, as the present anecdotal evidence that doing so induces a more tree-like habit makes classifying plants from their growth habits very difficult.

M. × loebneri was the subject of an excellent review by Graham Rankin in the 1999 Yearbook and will not be further discussed here, so it remains to examine the best varieties of *M. stellata*.

Cultivars of *M. stellata* listed in the *RHS Plant Finder*

We should start with cultivars so listed as there is little more frustrating to have a plant recommended and then to find it is impossible to obtain. It will be clear to the attentive reader that, because of the variation in the wild plants, there can be no such thing as a typical *M. stellata* from a taxonomic viewpoint, but it is still obviously important to know what can be expected of the "*M. stellata*" purchased in a garden centre, so let's refer to this as *M. stellata* of gardens.

In spite of all the more modern varieties, *M. stellata* of gardens remains a very desirable plant and should be in every garden; it seems that plants purchased under this label stand a good chance of being small and bush like, of moderate growth rates when young, and slower later. Avoid plants showing an obvious leader if a bush is required, and, for the reasons mentioned earlier, avoid grafted plants. *M. stellata* of gardens will flower young, and the flowers will be white, scented, at least 10cm (4in) across, and are likely to have 12–18 tepals. It will flower at the beginning of the season, typically in early April (mid-March in 2002) in the south of England, with a peak flowering season of three weeks, but with flowers showing for up to ten weeks[14]. It should attain a size or about 1.5m (5ft) tall by 3m (10ft) in ten years. An impression of the variations in such plants can be gained by visiting the Sir Harold Hillier Gardens and Arboretum near Winchester where over a dozen are planted near each other.

'**Centennial**' is a superb cultivar listed by four suppliers in the *RHS Plant Finder*. It is a seedling of *M. rosea*, raised at the Arnold Arboretum and originally known as 'Harvard Centennial' and, although it is said sometimes to have pink shades, it stands out for me as a white. The fragrant flowers are large – up to 14cm (5½in) across – with an average of about 20 tepals, and the plant's only drawback is that it is quite upright and vigorous, having reached a height of 4m (12ft) and a spread of 2.5m (8ft) in ten years in Sussex.

'**Chrysanthemiflora**' is a clone made very desirable by Sir Peter Smithers when he showed a slide of it at Vincent Square years ago, but plants I have seen with this label at Windsor and Wisley have been disappointing. Although they were very double with upwards of 25 tepals, they had only small, pale pink flowers. There seems to be some confusion in the trade with 'Jane Platt', perhaps because this is double and flowers late, at about the same time as 'Chrysanthemiflora', which is listed by Spinner's nursery[16].

'**Jane Platt**' is by far the best pink clone proven under UK conditions as its flowers remain pink until they fall. It is double in appearance with an average 26 tepals, quite vigorous, and seems to want to produce a leader and become a small tree. In my garden its growth rate at a ten year height of 3.5m (12ft) shows no sign of slowing (see Fig.15). It is later flowering than the type. The named plant originated in Portland, Oregon in the garden of the late Jane Platt, but a plant obtained by Sir Peter Smithers from Wada in Japan, and a clone named 'Keiskei Flore Pleno' have both turned out to be the same. It is available from Spinners and Dunge Valley[17].

'**Keiskei**' is listed in the *RHS Plant Finder* and there are photographs of both on Eisenhut's and Rutten's websites. Unfortunately they show different flowers. The confusion is made worse by the fact that a clone called 'Keiskei Flore Pleno' was listed by the Duchy of Cornwall nurseries some years ago, but there is no record of this plant in the literature and it is 'Jane Platt'. Some authorities regard 'Keiskei' itself as the same as the Wada clone of *M. rubra*. It seems that the clone available in the UK from Endsleigh Gardens is the double form, in which case it is likely to be 'Jane Platt', but Sherwood Cottage are selling a single pale form from Sir John Quicke's garden like the one on Rutten's list.

Confused? Do not purchase this variety without seeing its flower!

'**King Rose**' is almost certainly the same as 'King Rosea' and 'Rosea King', and may be the same as 'Rosea Massey' (which is listed separately in the *RHS Plant Finder*), 'Massey Rosea' and 'Dr Massey', the dark pink line mentioned by some authors as a distinguishing feature being variable from season to season. In any case all the names are misleading, as the flower has rose shades only in bud and then very pale, and opens to white with

25–30 tepals on a bush that tends to become tree like, being quite vigorous – 3m (10ft) tall and wide in ten years for me. It seems to have originated in New Zealand. It flowers slightly later than *M. stellata*, but earlier than 'Jane Platt'. It is an excellent and floriferous garden plant, but it is not rose.

'**Rosea**' (also 'Rose') has been in cultivation for many years, clones being separately imported into Europe and the USA before 1900. More than one clone is almost certainly in circulation in both continents. The name is misleading, as the pink colour is only reliably present in bud, and fades out as the flower opens in most years. Under unusual weather conditions, usually after a mild short winter such as 2001–2 the colour is stronger, and is likely to be stronger in countries with climates like southern Switzerland. Habit and tepal number are similar to the typical white *M. stellata*.

'**Royal Star**' is a seedling of 'Waterlily' and has the palest pink buds opening to a beautiful white flower with an average of 20 tepals. This clone is very floriferous, and has a slightly more upright habit than typical. A superb clone.

'**Waterlily**' is an excellent white clone introduced to commerce in the UK by Hilliers. The flowers are large and have an average of 24 tepals. The plant will make a well-shaped and stately bush of 1.5m (5ft) by 3m (10ft) in ten years.

M. stellata cultivars not listed in the *RHS Plant Finder*, but available through mail order from continental Europe

'**Alixeed**' is reported to be a new light pink cultivar of *M. stellata*, but it is not recorded whether the colour fades out as the flowers develop. It originated as an open-pollinated seedling in Indiana and is reported to be quite fragrant with sturdy flowers, which remain upright and bears 'lots' of tepals. It is said to be a vigorous grower and becomes a small, single-stemmed tree, reaching 4.5m (13ft) in twelve years, so may be a *M.* × *loebneri* cultivar. It is now available from Rutten.

'Dawn' is an American clone listed by Eisenhut[3], with pink, almost double flowers. It sounds desirable but appears not to be in cultivation in the UK[13].

'F55' is a pink clone listed by Eisenhut. In his photograph it appears to have 16 tepals.

'Green Star' is another American clone having an intriguing name, which makes it sound very exciting. When first opening, flowers have a thin line of yellowish green down the middle of some of the tepals, but it is no improvement on clones generally available[15]. It is not available in Europe at present.

'Kikuzaki' is a clone similar to the common *M. stellata*, but with 20–30 tepals on small flowers, which are initially pink and borne in great numbers on young plants. It is almost certainly a wild clone introduced from a Japanese nursery to the USA, but it is becoming available in Europe, and there is a picture on Rutten's website[2]. It is probably not worth seeking out except for its early floriferousness; it flowers at the same time as, or slightly earlier than *M. stellata*, but it is not so long lasting.

'Rubra' has been called 'Red Star' in the US, and is another moveable feast with more than one clone in cultivation. The one commonest in the USA originated from Wada, who described it in 1925 as 'a very fine form with deep rosy pink flowers, well retaining its bright colour until flowers fade, forms a small tree ultimately.' Another form with this name was raised in Holland before 1948 from a batch of *M. stellata* seedlings, and it is probably

this form that is usual in the UK. Janaki Anmal suggested from its chromosome count (2n=51, compared to 38 for *M. stellata*) that this was a hybrid. In any case, the name 'Rubra' is flattering, as, although darker than *M. rosea*, it is merely pale pink, but does have a darker stripe on the outside of the tepals. Flowers on the few plants I have seen defy nursery catalogue descriptions by fading as the flowers open. It is later flowering than most other cultivars.

'Scented Silver' is yet another of those American plants with desirable-sounding names. It is said to be white without any tint of colour and is quite fragrant. The original plant is 25 or more years old and grows as a single bole tree; it is taller than it is wide. Selected in 1973 and registered in 1990 by Frank Galyon from Tennessee, who reports that it 'has the most incredible pleasant lemony fragrance of all Asiatic Magnolias.' The plant in Sir John Quicke's garden in Sherwood apparently lives up to the description of a pleasant scent without being outstanding. It is listed by Eisenhut.

'Waterlily' is a name given to a number of differing American clones, said to be pink. I have not been able to identify any in the UK so far, though doubtless they exist.

Polyploid forms

'Norman Gould' FCC 1967 is a colchicine-induced polyploid form familiar to most British enthusiasts as it was raised at Wisley by Janaki Anmal. Treseder[12] states the commonly held opinion that Norman Gould arose from treatment of *M. stellata* seed, but Gardiner[13] treats it as a form of *M. kobus*. This must be correct as the original plant on Battleston Hill at Wisley is now a good-sized tree, with other very high-quality large trees from the same treatment growing around it, and Anmal was only likely to have access to

M. kobus seed[18]. The Anmal plants therefore lie outside the scope of this article.

'Two Stones' is a genuine colchicine-induced tetraploid developed from *M. stellata* by Augie Kehr in the US. It has thicker and larger leaves and tepals with some doubling in a most attractive flower. It is listed by Rutten, and is reputed to have compact growth.

Hybrids of recent introduction that should be considered by anyone contemplating a collection of *M. stellata*-like cultivars.

'Gold Star' is an American hybrid with *M. acuminata*. The creamy yellow, star-like flowers are up to 10cm (4in) wide, appearing just before the foliage, and have 14 strap-shaped tepals, thus creating a cream *M. stellata*, but one with flowers not of the quality of other *M. stellata* specimens. (See Fig.14). It grows quickly, and at least when young shows the bushy side-branching of *M. stellata*, but a plant at Wisley is following its *M. acuminata* parent and rapidly turning into a large tree. Of course it might be possible to keep 'Goldstar' small by removing any leaders it forms while still young. The leaves have a wonderful red tinge when young, so overall this clone is very desirable, and it is now readily available in the UK.

'Pink Perfection' is an American selection of *M.* × *loebneri*, the result of a self-cross of 'Encore'. It only comes within the scope of this article as it is said to be a very bushy tree, slow-growing to almost dwarf. The flowers are lilac-pink and have 42–58 tepals. There is a photograph on the Dunge Valley website[16], and the clone is available from them as well as being on Eisenhut's list.

'Stellar Acclaim' is another *M. acuminata* hybrid, and similar to *M.* 'Butterflies' except that the tepals are narrower and they open to the *M. stellata* form lying flat along the branches. They are approximately 10cm (4in) wide in my garden. The growth habit is bushy to 1.5m (5ft) high by 2m (6ft) across in eight years. Once again it can be seen on the Dunge Valley website[16].

'Stardust' is a little-known plant raised by Amos Pickard of Canterbury among a batch of *M.* 'Picture' seedlings. It has the *M. kobus* leaf type. The flowers are somewhat like *M. stellata* but larger, with an ivory tinge, and do not open flat. My plant, in a poor position, has remained small. The sight of the elegantly poised flowers on the naked branches in spring make this universally admired, and it is a clone that should be better known. It is listed by Rutten.

A personal view

I think the clones of *M. stellata* rank very high in the list of shrubby magnolias, but if I had to choose just two would go for *M. stellata* itself, because of its growth habit, and 'Jane Platt' as by far the best pink. They would be followed by 'Waterlily', 'Centennial', 'Goldstar' and 'Stardust', and a wild-collected seedling for that exciting anticipation, shared by all plantsmen and women.

Acknowledgements

I am grateful, among others, to the ever-cheerful Jim Gardiner for his assistance in preparing this article.

References

[1] MAGNOLIA SOCIETY. Checklist of cultivars. www.magnoliasociety.org
[2] RUTTEN, Wim. www.magnoliastore.com
[3] EISENHUT, Vivaio. www.eisenhut.ch
[4] LORD, Tony (Ed). *The RHS Plant Finder*. Dorling Kindersley. www.rhs.org.uk/rhs-plantfinder/plantfinder.asp

[5]BLACKBURN, J. *New York Botanic Garden* (1952), 53.

[6]CALLAWAY, D. *The World of Magnolias.*

[7]SPONGBERG, S. (1998). *Magnolias and their Allies,* 123–4.

[8]OHBA, Hideaki. (1998) *Magnolias and their allies,* 155–9.

[9]JAPANESE ASSOCIATION OF SHIDEKOBUSHI CONSERVATION (1996). *Wild stand of Shidekobushi in Japan,* 217.

[10]GARDINER J. (June, 2002) *The Plantsman,* 76

[11]VAN GELDEREN, DE JONG, and OTERDOOM (1994). *Maples of the World,* 235.

[12]TRESEDER, N. (1978). *Magnolias,* 165.

[13]GARDINER, J. (2000). *Magnolias – A Gardener's Guide,* 190.

[14]DE SPOELBERCH, P. Unpublished Database of Magnolias at Herkenrode, Belgium.

[15]HERJE, S. Private communication.

[16]SPINNERS GARDENS AND NURSERY, Boldre, Hampshire.

[17]DUNGE VALLEY HIDDEN GARDENS, www.dunge valley.co.uk

[18]GARDINER, J. Private communication.

Michael Robinson is Chairman of the South-east Branch of the Group and gardens in the Ashdown Forest. He is an active member of The Magnolia Society

Ghent Azaleas:
Fig. 10 (above): Azalea 'Pontica Chromatella' (see p.35).
Fig. 11 (right): Azalea 'Van Houtte Flore Pleno' (see p.35). Fig. 12 (below): Azalea 'Standishii' (see p.35)
Fig. 13 (below right): Azalea 'Bijou de Gentbrugge' (see p.35)

Fig. 14 (above): Magnolia stellata *'Goldstar'* at Hindleap Lodge, East Sussex (see p.47).
Fig. 15 (left): Magnolia stellata *'Jane Platt'* at Hindleap Lodge, East Sussex (see p.44).
Fig. 16 (below): Magnolia stellata *at Gilu, Japan showing flower variation (see p.42).*

Bulbous Plants to Grow with Rhododendrons, Camellias and Magnolias:
Fig. 17 (left): Trillium chloropetalum *white at Spinners (see p.56).*
Fig. 18 (above): Lilium macklinae *at Spinners (see p.59).*
Fig. 19 (below): Erythronium *'White Beauty' at Spinners (see p.57).*

Photographic Competition (see p.84):
Fig 20 (left): The winner of the £25 first
prize – Magnolia sieboldii *taken by Mr*
J.G. Rees.
Fig. 21 (above): Second place was given to
Mr. C. Waddington's R. lindleyi.
Fig. 22 (below): Third place went to Dr
G. B. Hargreave's Magnolia sprengeri *var.*
diva, *taken at Westonbirt.*

A Home for Forgotten Beauties

Cynthia Postan

The collection of old varieties of rhododendrons at Ramster[1] should be high on everyone's list of gardens to be visited. Not only is it much more than a mere collection of flowering shrubs, which in their time were passionately admired for their brilliant colours, but because for more than 100 years they have provided the main structure of many important gardens in this country. The decorative potentiality of the genus came to be recognised in the late 18th and early 19th Centuries with the arrival of two species from the East Coast of the USA (*R. maximum* in 1736 and *R. catawbiense* in 1809) to be joined by others from Europe (*R. ponticum* in 1763, *R. caucasicum* in 1809 and *R. dauricum* in 1780) and India (*R. campanulatum* in 1825, *R. barbatum* in 1829 and *R. arboreum* (in 1809). It was not long before those gardeners interested in improving wild species saw how this (to them) exotic plant material might be used in gardens. The early years of rhododendron breeding have been told by Lionel de Rothschild the younger[2]. But before the genus could make its full impact on the garden scene, certain readily apparent weaknesses had to be eradicated. Here the work of both amateur and professional gardeners combined to produce the vivid colours and to prevent the flowers being ruined by the treacherous frosts of April and May.

Colour came from the Himalayas; frost evasion from the Pontic-Americans. How these two characteristics came to be combined and the progeny to dominate the gardens of the Home Counties was the handiwork of the skill and imagination of both amateurs and nurserymen. The plants themselves are known to us today as the Hardy Hybrids.

The Hardy Hybrids

Perhaps the best definition of Hardy Hybrids is Desmond Clarke's in J.S.Bean's great tome:

> [They are] a group of nursery-bred rhododendrons, mostly many generations removed from the wild parents, which are very hardy, flower mostly in late May or June, tolerate exposure and full sun, and bear firm, upright, many-flowered trusses in a wide range of colouring. They owe their toughness to members of the Ponticum series, but the colouring... comes mainly from *R. arboreum* and the dense, many-flowered truss of this species has also helped to give the Hardy Hybrids their distinct floral characters.[3]

Within a few years of its first flowering in 1825, *R. arboreum* was being crossed with Pontic-Americans, but it was not until these hybrids were back crossed onto their hardy parents that colour could be combined with late flowering. Other significant parents were *R. campanulatum* and *R. griffithianum*, the latter introduced by Sir Joseph Hooker in 1849. From the 1850s onwards, to quote Desmond Clarke again, "Hardy Hybrids were in 'full spate' and in the next two or three decades 'most of the varieties known today made their appearance'". Although amateur gardeners, such as James and Henry Mangles, and great landowners, such as the earls of Carnarvon and Liverpool through their gardeners and friends, not to mention the Cornish families of Fox and Shilson and their gardeners, played a part in attempts to improve the garden-worthiness of rhododendrons, the next phase of hybridisation passed inevitably into the hands of the nursery trade.

In those early days there were many nursery gardens whose names are all but forgotten now but who bear an honorable place in the history of hybridisation. The list of plants at Ramster contains names that were bred by such firms as Fisher, Sons & Sibray of Sheffield, Cunningham & Frazer of Comely Bank, Methvens of Edinburgh, Isaac Davies of Ormskirk, Lee & Kennedy of Hammersmith and others known only to historians of nursery gardens. There were also nursery gardens on the continent of Europe who joined in the hybridising game. The best known and the oldest is the family firm of T.J. Seidel Brothers of Dresden, who produced a dynasty lasting several generations. Their connection with rhododendrons dates back to the early 1800s. In fact the first member of the family, Johann Heinrich Seidel (1744–1815), a German by birth, was a defector from Napoleon's army on its march to Moscow. Their lovely pure white hybrid 'Helene Schiffner' is at Ramster. There were other well-known nursery gardens specialising in rhododendrons and azaleas in Belgium (Van Houtte) and Holland (Van Nes, Koster and Kluis), all of them also worthily represented at Ramster.

The Surrey Nurseries

But the main stream of new varieties undoubtedly came from nurseries in one small area in Surrey whose names have become almost synonymous with the words Hardy Hybrid. The best known of these produced the dynasties (appropriately so described) of Waterer and Slocock, although the short-lived nursery partnership of Standish & Noble was for a time influential. The latter's nursery grounds were later to become famous through the name of Sunningdale.

As long ago as 1850 the Gardeners' Chronicle described the Surrey home of the rhododendron in somewhat lurid terms, as lying:

> in the midst of a bleak barren common without shelter or shade, exposed to the burning heat of summer and open to the rude blasts of winter, and suffering both from early frosts in autumn and late ones in spring… [here] the finest American plants are grown for sale.[4]

These were the marginal lands of the former Windsor Forest. The soil, a mixture of Bracklesham Loam and Bagshot Sand, was unsuitable for farming, though less expensive than lands nearer the capital[5]. However, the standard of cultivation at Waterer's nurseries was always very high[6]. The area, centred on Woking, highly significant for its later development, lay across the Portsmouth Road, along which no less than 30 coaches a day passed. Later, a branch railway was even considered to cope with what was to become a vast trade.

The most important of these nurseries, and one that has survived until today, at least by name, is, of course, Knaphill, the original home since the 18th Century of the Waterer family. The family firm became a limited company in 1924 and has eventually joined forces with another dynasty, the Slococks of Old Goldsworth. The latter family came on the scene later, in the middle of the 19th Century. But between them these two families were responsible for producing more named varieties than any other nursery and played a major part in the diaspora of the rhododendron. Many of the varieties they bred in the latter half of the 19th Century are still available, although the collection at Ramster contains some which are even older[7].

The Waterers of Knaphill and Bagshot

The story of the Waterer family relates to four generations of men with a strong dedication to their chosen calling and an equally strong competitive spirit. We can readily associate it with the vigorous entrepreneurial energy of the Victorian age. The family had been established at Ryde Heron in the 18th Century, but the individuals to whom we owe most of the collection at Ramster were (to borrow Lionel II's 'regal' differentiation of the various family members):

Michael I (1745–1827); **Michael II** (1770–1842); **John I,** Michael II's brother (1794–1868); **John II,** John I's son (1826–93); **John III,** John IIs son (1865–1948); **Gomer,** also John II's son (1867–1945); **Hosea I,** another of John I's sons (1793–1853); **Anthony I,** Michael I's nephew (1822–96); **Anthony II,** Anthony I's son (1850–1924); **Hosea II,** the American member of the family (1852–1926).

The nurseries themselves were at Knaphill and nearby Bagshot. In their 1869 catalogue, the nurseries were described as covering 200 acres of which 60 were devoted to the 'American' plants (i.e. rhododendrons and azaleas)[8]. Between February and December 1894 (when the nursery was at its most prolific), 180 different named varieties were sold as well as 800 plants whose names were not recorded. Almost every well-known nursery in the country were among the customers. To give an idea of the scale of the trade in the 'lifting' season, it is recorded that in the 1860s up to 10 tons (of plants) were carried by wagon each day to the nearest railway station for despatch all over the country and even overseas as far as India and the USA – where Hosea I had established a very profitable connection.[8]

All the members of the family mentioned above were at one time or another nominal owners of the two nurseries, which varied according to the testamentary dispositions of the head of the family at the time. They sometimes traded separately but ultimately were reunited under one management. We are told by J.G. Millais, in his great book published in 1917 that they had (by then) introduced 292 varieties, all of them 'hardy' in the horticultural sense of the word.[9] However, the successful breeders, although they knew nothing of genetics, would have had strong personal theories based on an intimate knowledge of their individual plants. The choice of seed or pollen parents and selected forms were generally acknowledged to be all important.[10] For instance, Anthony I had a fondness for blotched and speckled flowers derived from *R. maximum*. According to P.D. Williams (quoted by Lionel II, to use his own categorisation), Anthony I relied principally on hybridisation, while Anthony II preferred to breed by selection. Hosea I wished to concentrate on late flowering. One striking feature of the Waterer family was that of secrecy. In such a competitive world, details of parentage were jealously guarded. A typical example is that of 'Pink Pearl', which swept the board for John II and Gomer in 1894. The most the propagator would ever admit to was that one parent 'might have been *R. griffithianum*'.[11] Both Frederick Street and Lionel II, in their accounts, stress this feature, Lionel II even commenting on the use of the p words – 'perhaps, probably, possibly, putative' when attributing parentage. This means that the hardy hybrid connoisseur of today is at liberty to make his own surmises.

Of the plants at Ramster the following can be assigned to individual members of the family. They are:

Michael I: 'Sappho', 'Lady Clementine Mitford', 'Lady Annette de Trafford', 'Mrs R. S. Holford'.

Michael II: 'Cetewayo', 'Nobleanum'.

John I: 'Alice', 'Gomer Waterer', 'Lady Eleanor Cathcart', 'John Walter'.

John 11: 'Bagshot Ruby', 'Mrs E.C. Stirling', 'Pink Pearl'.

Anthony I: 'Everestianum', 'Doncaster', 'Lady Grey Egerton', 'Caractacus'.

Anthony II: 'Purple Splendour', 'Mrs Davies Evans', 'J.C.Williams', 'Mrs Furnivall', 'Mrs J.G. Millais'.

Gomer: 'Blue Danube', 'Blue Peter', 'Corona', 'Starfish', 'Sweet Simplicity'.

Standish & Noble

The brief partnership of Standish & Noble at Sunningdale (and, after it was dissolved in 1857, at the Royal Ascot Nursery) is remembered at Ramster by some notable varieties: 'Cynthia', 'Ascot Brilliant', 'The Bride', 'Caucasicum Pictum', to name but a few. Standish had been hybridising from as early as 1838 with 'Blandyanum' (not at Ramster), and the nursery is said to have received through John Lindley's influence Robert Fortune's Chinese seedlings, the only important one for us being *R. fortunei*. The breakup of this great partnership is famously remembered by Standish's saying, 'The sun cannot shine on two horizons'. Noble continued at Sunningdale, which

had a great revival in the 20th Century under the management of Harry White and James Russell, before the latter removed his best plants to Castle Howard. One variety, 'Lady Longman', is represented at Ramster along with the 'Countess of Derby', which is said to be very similar to 'Pink Pearl'.[12]

The Slococks of Old Goldsworth

Goldsworth as a nursery dates back in the records to the late 1700s, but its great days began when Walter Charles Slocock took over. He was born in 1854 and died in 1926, and seems always to have known where his destiny lay. From 1869 he worked at Knaphill for Anthony Waterer I who is said to have taken a personal interest in him and to have given him specially responsible tasks with hybrids. Later his movements took him to work at Fraser's of Woodford and to Van Houtte in Belgium (both azalea specialists) before coming back in 1877 to England to Goldsworth Old Nursery. He bought the goodwill on borrowed capital, acquired another 24 acres on mortgage and by 1890 had 300 acres with sales amounting to £13,820. He was a good business man, but also a hard worker often working from 8 in the morning until 10 at night, and riding round the nursery on his old cob. His ability to get on with others and his bluff hail-fellow-well-met manner were remembered by his neighbour and biographer, John Street. He is also famous for his notebooks, started when he was a young man at Knaphill in which he recorded his life's work. He was succeeded by his sons, Walter Ashley (1896–1963) and Oliver Charles (1907–70), both in his own image, and by his grandson, Martin, until last year Treasurer of the Royal Horticultural Society. All generations of the family have long been associated with the RHS and its Shows.[13]

The long list of the Slocock introductions is well represented at Ramster, and includes 'Mount Everest', 'Susan', 'Butterfly', 'Goldsworth Yellow', 'James Burchett' (after their long-term foreman), 'Lavender Girl', 'Mrs W.C. Slocock', 'Unique' and 'Letty Edwards'.

There is a certain poetic justice that the name of these two great families should finally come together in 1976 at Knaphill, within 300–400 yards of Ryde Heron the original home of the Waterers. Between them they had made Surrey the capital of the genus and filled our gardens with what we might well call "The Summer Queen". The late Lord Aberconway has aptly described the 'well-filled truss of the Bagshot catalogue'.[14] Jack Frost's icy fingers had been well and truly frustrated. It was left to the tender hybrids with their 'showers of drooping bells' to flourish elsewhere. Perhaps, as has been noted in another place, this represents the main disparity of approach between the great gardeners and the great nurserymen.

Notes

[1] GUNN, M. and BOND, J. (2000). The Hardy Hybrid Rhododendron Collections, *Rhododendrons with Camellias and Magnolias*, No. 51, p.55, and 'The Groups' Plant Collections', *ibid* (2001) No.52, p.52.

[2] DE ROTHSCHILD, L. (1996). *The Rhododendrons Story* (Ed. C. Postan), p. 115–35. (To differentiate him from his grandfather of the same name, Lionel is referred to throughout as Lionel II).

[3] BEAN, J.D. (1976). *Trees and Shrubs Hardy in the British Isles,* 8th Edition. Vol.III (Ed. D. Clarke), p.817.

[4] WILLSON, E.J. (1989) *Nurserymen to the World* (1989), p.9.

[5] *Ibid,* p.1.

[6] BEAN, J.D. *loc. cit.* 'Additional Notes' by D. Waterer, p.937. 'The standard of cultivation in both Knaphill and Bagshot Nurseries was extremely high. Meticulous attention was paid to land drainage, to soil fertility and to the eradication of disease.' Farms were maintained (as also at Slocock's Goldsworth Nursery) to provide manure and replace soil lost when rooted plants were dug up for sale.

[7] STREET, F. (1954). *Hardy Rhododendrons.* p.31 lists the following hybrids, which are represented at Ramster as being more than 75 years old at that time (now, of course, more than 125 years old): 'Chionoides', 'Cynthia', 'Doncaster', 'Everestianum', 'Fastuosum Flore Pleno', 'John Walter', 'Lady Annette de Trafford', 'Lady Clementine Mitford', 'Lady Grey Egerton', 'Sappho'.

[8] WILLSON. *loc. cit* pp. 12–15 and *passim,* quoting D. Waterer in Bean, *loc. cit.*

[9] MILLAIS, J.G. (1917). *Rhododendrons,* Part I. Quoted in Rothschild, *loc.cit.* p.130.

[10] The classic example is that of the parentage of 'Loderi', a cross between *R. fortunei* and *R. griffithianum*. The pollen of the latter from F.D. Godman's garden at South Lodge was taken to neighbouring Leonardslee and applied to a good form of *R. fortunei*. A similar cross with inferior forms had been made earlier at Kew and was not so successful.

[11] STREET, *loc. cit.* p.28, quoting W. Watson (1912) *Rhododendrons and Azaleas,* p. 37.

[12] WILLSON, *loc. cit.* Chap.6; J. Russell (1960) *Rhododendrons at Sunningdale.*

[13] WILLSON, *loc. cit.* Chap.4.

[14] ROTHSCHILD, *loc. cit.* p.125.

References

BEAN, W. J. (1976). *Trees & Shrubs Hardy in the British Isles*, part III, 8th Edn (Ed. Desmond Clarke), pp.539–940. John Murray.

COX, Peter A. & Kenneth (1988). *Encyclopedia of Rhododendron Hybrids*. Batsford.

GREER, H. (1982). *Harold Greer's Guidebook to available Rhododendron Species and Hybrids*.

GUNN, M & BOND, J. (2000 & 2001) The Hardy Hybrid Collection. *Rhododendrons with Camellias & Magnolias*, Nos.51 & 52. RHS.

MILLAIS, J.G. (1917 & 1924). *Rhododendrons and their various Hybrids*, 2 Vols. Longmans, Green.

POSTAN, Cynthia (ed) (1996). *The Rhododendron Story. 200 Years of Plant Hunting and Garden Cultivation*. RHS.

ROTHSCHILD, Lionel (1996). Hybrids in the British Isles: the 19th Century. *The Rhododendron Story*. RHS.

RUSSELL, James (1960). *Rhododendrons at Sunningdale*. Sunningdale Nurseries.

STREET, Frederick (1954). *Hardy Rhododendrons*. Van Nostrand & Garden Book-Club.

WATERER, Donald (1976). The Waterers and Standish & Noble. In W.J. Bean *Trees & Shrubs Hardy in the British Isles*, p.934.

WATSON, William (1912). *Rhododendrons & Azaleas*. J.C. & E.C. Jack.

WILLSON, Eleanor J. (1989). *Nurserymen to the World: the Nursery Gardens of Woking and North-West Surrey and Plants introduced by them*. Willson.

Lady Cynthia Postan is an Honorary Life Member of the Group and for ten years Hon Editor of the Yearbook. In 1996 she edited the Group's publication The Rhododendron Story

BULBOUS PLANTS TO GROW WITH RHODODENDRONS, MAGNOLIAS AND CAMELLIAS

KEVIN HUGHES

Throughout their range these trees and shrubs occur together with an enormous and a diverse range of bulbous flora, whether they be crocuses in the Caucasus, trilliums in the USA or arisaemas in Asia (I use bulbous as a loose term to cover rhizomes, corms, tubers, bulbs, etc). In the garden, therefore, it is no surprise that bulbous plants make very suitable companion planting for rhododendrons, magnolias and camellias. Unless you include the release of nutrients from a bulbous plant's foliage prior to its dormancy, it is hard to see how they can offer benefits to the shrubs and trees. The gardener, however, can use his shrubs to create habitat for them.

Deciduous magnolias and rhododendrons provide the greatest opportunities for associating with bulbs. The majority of woodland bulbous plants are programmed to grow during the autumn to spring period when many shrubs and trees will be without leaves. Most of these will also appreciate the organic rich soils that the subject trees and shrubs enjoy. America is the centre of diversity for two genera that are particular favourites of mine: trilliums and erythroniums.

Many trilliums hail from neutral or alkaline soils but all except *Trillium nivale*

will thrive in acid conditions. Trilliums grow from rhizomes but are sometimes described as herbaceous magnolias because of a certain visual similarity in their flowers. A few species are found in China and Japan, but America is home to the most exciting members of the genus. Typically they are part of the woodland flora and in gardens relish the 'windbreaks' provided by shrubs and the dappled shade cast by trees. In the eastern USA they can be found growing in the company of both magnolias and rhododendrons. The most exotic, and the first to bloom, are the sessile species with flowers that emerge directly from the three bracts (leaves). *T. chloropetalum* and its close cousins *T. kurabayashii* and *T. albidum* from western America are plants I would find it hard to be without. Their foliage is bold and often heavily marked in a tapestry of dark blotches – flowering occurs from March to May. They can be big architectural plants; *T. chloropetalum giganteum* 'Spinners' can reach 50cm (20in) in height, the heavily patterned bracts of each peduncle spreading 30cm (12in) and its wine red flowers lasting over six weeks before fading. The colour of this cultivar is typical of its species and the very similar *T. kurabayashii*. These two species are so close that they are very difficult to separate without known provenance and readily hybridise when grown together, resulting in a lot of confusion about the identity of many garden populations. There is an especially garden-worthy cultivar of *T. chloropetalum* that is particularly beautiful, but is possibly a natural hybrid with *T. albidum*, distributed under the name *T. chloropetalum* white (see Fig.17). Its flowers are large with pink bases to the white petals with a rose-like fragrance and last several weeks before fading.

Eastern America is home to the greatest diversity of sessile species (17 species). Not all make good garden plants. *T. discolor*, for instance, has pale yellow petals enhanced by dark anther connectives, creating a subtly beautiful flower, but in European gardens it is frequently decimated by slugs. A much better subject is *T. cuneatum*, superficially similar to *T. chloropetalum* but with a greater diversity of foliage patterns ranging from rare silver forms to others where the dark blotches are so closely packed that the bracts appear almost black. Like most sessile species it generally flowers between March and April. The flowers of *T. luteum* generally open a week or so later than *T. cuneatum* and its foliage is lighter green and more subtle. This suits its yellow, lemon-scented flowers, though their fragrance is only apparent at close range or on warm days.

The pedicelate species with flowers supported above or below the bracts on a pedicel tend to emerge a little later than their sessile relatives. Perhaps the best of these is the eastern 'wake robin', *T. grandiflorum*, which usually begins to flower in April although some forms don't bloom until mid-May. It has large, showy white or pink flowers and when seen *en masse* these can rival

the spectacle of any magnolia. *T. ovatum* from western America is very similar in appearance but with more defined obovate petals (mostly lanceolate to oblong in *T. grandiflorum*). In gardens it often flowers a little earlier than *T. grandiflorum*, although many gardeners find that if they can grow one well the other sulks. Some gardeners in the southeastern USA have difficulty in growing *T. ovatum* or indeed any of the western USA species. In Spinners' garden in southern Britain this has long been the case. *T. grandiflorum* has formed a good-sized colony but *T. ovatum*, mostly Californian stock, failed to establish itself. Now, however, a recent introduction of *T. ovatum* from Portland, Oregon appears to be bucking the trend and growing well so it can sometimes pay to keep trying. Rather different is *T. sulcatum*. This is a tall species. Its flowers with purplish, sometimes almost black, reflexed petals are held up proudly on a long pedicel. *T. vaseyi* is a shy but very beautiful species. It also tends to the purplish colours, although rare white forms occur and its broad-petalled flowers can be twice as big as those of *T. sulcatum*. Unfortunately it hides them beneath its bracts and so ideally it should be planted on a bank where you can look up at it. Many are supplied to the trade from the wild and apart from the ethical considerations these have a poor record in gardens. This is in large part due to poor storage resulting in dehydration of the rhizomes and loss of roots. These dormant rhizomes may also be carrying fungal diseases that will not become apparent until growth starts in the spring. For best results obtain only cultivated specimens, although you may have to pay a little more, and protect newly planted stock from slugs.

In contrast to trilliums, erythroniums are ephemeral beauties, with individual flowers lasting as little as a week. Most will thrive in well-drained woodland soils and do not mind if they dry out somewhat during the summer. Europe has one species, *Erythronium dens-canis* (with a range extending into Asia) that comes in white and pink forms and starts flowering in March. Some of the large-flowered eastern forms or species such as *E. sibiricum* and *E. japonicum* are especially beautiful when growing well but with me their vulnerability to slugs has led to their failure in the garden. Like most members of the genus, *E. dens-canis* has pendent flowers with upwardly reflexed perianth segments from which extend prominent anthers.

The gems of the genus come from western America. *E. revolutum* opens in April with graceful flowers in every shade of pink. It has yellow anthers and superb foliage marbled in hues of brownish purple and cream. Once established, allow it to seed itself around and after about ten years you can have hundreds of flowering bulbs. Superficially similar, and certainly as beautiful with delicate lilac petals and purple anthers, is *E. hendersonii,* which flowers in March. Equally desirable are the closely related *E. californicum* and *E. oregonum*. These are both elegant in appearance with cream flowers and mottled leaves and are reproduced mainly from seed. Carl Purdy, a Californian nurseryman selected *E.* 'White Beauty' (see Fig.19). It is thought to be a form of *E. californicum*, which it resembles in flower but it is a stockier plant and a good clumper, ideal for easy propagation. When planted in mixed groups, the preceding American species will readily hybridise with each other,

a point to bear in mind if you wish to retain the true species in your collection. *E. tuolumnense,* found locally in the Sierra Nevada, is acid yellow with unmarked foliage but can be shy to bloom. Its hybrid progeny such as Erythronium 'Pagoda', are a softer yellow, more generous with their favour and increase quickly. Two other growable yellow species are *E. americanum* and *E. umbilicatum* from the eastern USA. These closely resemble the European dog's tooth violet, *E. dens canis,* except in colour. The former will spread quickly by stolons but in some forms it can be shy to flower. You can encourage it by confining the bulbs between slates or by deep planting. The resulting congested clumps of bulbs will be freer with their flowers. The colour of a further species resembles a fried egg 'sunny-side up'. This is *E. multiscapoideum,* which in our garden in southern England is the first to bloom, coming out as early as February and lasting longer than most species, perhaps because of the cool temperatures at that time of year.

Some bulbs such as *Scilla, Crocus* and *Cyclamen* spp are vulnerable to the attention of rodents. If these are planted into the fibrous roots of deciduous rhododendrons or the fleshy roots of magnolias they gain a measure of protection, the roots acting as an organic chicken wire. *Fritillaria* spp are aided in the same way. Many are alpine house subjects, but there are some good species suited to the open garden and most flower in the spring. Perhaps the best (it would be highly prized indeed if it came from an obscure mountain in Tibet) is the European *F. meleagris* or 'snakeshead fritillary'. Naturally occurring in meadows, it adapts well to a woodland garden where it will often naturalise. Like most species it appreciates good drainage. Its pendant, usually single, lantern-shaped flowers are held on stems about 35cm (14in) tall and are either pale lilac-purple, with strong darker toned tessellations, or white. *F. pyrenaica* from Spain and the Pyrenees grows about the same height but has much darker flowers coloured yellowish inside. There is also a good yellow form, var. *lutescens*. From Asia come the pale yellow *F. pallidiflora* and the black *F. camschatcensis*, the latter also occurring in north west America and Canada. Both are superb woodland subjects but are rather vulnerable to the attentions of slugs and they require that mythical 'moist but well-drained soil'. Like many woodland bulbs they seem to appreciate the gradual drying out of the ground that starts with the onset of tree growth. *F. thunbergii* grows to about 1m (3ft) and its upper leaves have tendril-like tips with which it grasps other plants to gain extra support. Each stem on a well-grown plant supports five or six cream-coloured bells with a hint of green tessallation. An adaptable American species is *F. affinis,* which comes in a range of forms, usually with the expected dark tessellations giving it the name 'checker lily'. Plants from a tall- growing population (45cm/18in) from woodland near Eugene, Oregon where they occur with *Trillium parviflorum*, have proved excellent in the woodland garden at Spinners, flowering in April underneath and in the roots of various deciduous rhododendrons. This fritillary is typical of the more delicate species in its vulnerability to heavy mulches of leaf litter or bark through which the emergent shoots have difficulty penetrating making them more vulnerable to ambush by slugs. Heavy mulches can also smother newly germinating seedlings of

Fritillaria spp and many other bulbous subjects. Similar and even more vulnerable in this respect are *F. recurva* and *F. gentneri*. They originate in the western USA where they often occur in clay soils but in maritime Britain, in order to cultivate them in the open garden, these unusual red-flowered species require a well-drained position. A light mulch of pine needles seems to suit them well.

Closely related to fritillarias, *Lilium* spp are often easier to cultivate and because many flower in the summer they can add interest in one of the duller periods of the rhododendron/camellia season. A very natural look is created by allowing them to grow out of the front of smaller rhododendron just as they so often do in the wild. Many hybrid lilies have a weak constitution but primary hybrids and species are much tougher. The European 'turkscap' *L. martagon* will readily naturalise. It occurs in a range of colours and there have been some especially fine selections (almost black) of var. *cattaniae*, one of the best of these being Maurice Foster's 'The Moor'. From Turkey comes *L. monadelphum*, a pale yellow turkscap, that smells sweetly in the garden but if cut for the vase takes on the unpleasant odour of cats' urine in the confines of the house. Some American species from moist woodland produce flowers in vibrant shades of red, orange or yellow, often spotted with chocolate. They can look very good placed in front of rhododendrons with greyish young foliage such as *Rhododendron pseudochrysanthemum*. Among the easiest are *L. pardalinum* and the similar 'Bellingham Hybrids', both adaptable to a wide range of soils. The latter were raised by the US Department of Agriculture prior to 1933 and on good soils can be seen flowering in July on stems over 2m (6ft) tall. They can be very long-lived bulbs, with some clones being passed down through gardening families. *L. canadense* is especially beautiful but harder to please, demanding perfect drainage and acid, humus-rich soils that don't dry out too much. *L. superbum* is a species from the eastern USA. The inflorescence can support up to forty turkscap flowers held on stems over 2m (6ft) tall. The flowers are red at the petal tips, becoming orange-yellow towards the throat, which is spotted in chocolate. *L. superbum* is an adaptable species that naturally likes moist fertile soils and can survive winter flooding. On our poor soils at Spinners it only achieves 1.5m (5ft) in height at best and flowers in August. Introduced by Frank Kingdom-Ward from Burma *L. mackliniae* (see Fig.18) is a well-suited companion to dwarf rhododendrons. It likes peat-bed conditions and has elegant, shell pink flowers in May or June. Another good Asian species is *L. gloriosoides,* which displays its red-spotted, creamy white flowers in September. One hybrid I would not be without is *L.* 'Black Beauty'. In late summer its inflorescence of rich reddish purple 'turkscaps' are held at the end of leaning stems which can reach 2m (6ft), and it is one of the most resistant to lily beetle.

Finally the Asiatic *Arisaema* spp. or 'cobra lilies' are ideal companions. These aroids have weird and wonderful flowers that are always a conversation point in the garden. Some like *A. utile* and *A. griffithii* have flowers that take you back to childhood fantasies of dragons whilst a few have pretensions to beauty in the traditional sense. Of the former, *A. utile* has proved the better

plant with us. It is very similar to *A. griffithii* but that species seems to be rather ephemeral, going dormant after five weeks. *A. utile*, however, despite its slightly less sinister looking spathes, keeps its impressive foliage well into late summer. Its spathe is reddish brown with translucent white stripes, which allow light to shine through, a sort of stained-glass effect. *A. taiwanense* is another to look out for; its reddish brown spathes are out in May at the same time as its elegant, heavily dissected leaf, which is held like a sophisticated parasol above them. Altogether different is *A. dilatatum*, the petioles of its large leaves are whitish verrucose giving it a gunnera-like appearance. *A. speciosum* is a spectacular species with an indisputably tropical appearance, enhanced if associated with big-leaved rhododendrons such as *Rhododendron sinogrande*. It has reddish brown spathes and large, three-lobed leaves supported by petioles sometimes over 1m (3ft) in length and marked with a snakeskin pattern. Like *A. utile,* this species has a long season and can remain in leaf into the autumn. In colder districts it needs to be planted about 20cm (8in) deep to protect its tubers from winter freezes. For beauty, *A. candidissimum* cannot be beaten with its white spathes striped in green and pink. In our cool maritime climate it emerges from the ground late in the season, usually in June but sometimes in August. In the warmer southeast USA I have seen it out in March suggesting its flowering season is related to temperature. Like many in the genus, the spathes are followed by red berries. I find arisaemas appreciate a good feed whilst growing, a mulch of rotted dung being ideal, backed up with occasional applications of liquid seaweed.

Another genus that adds a tropical flavour to the garden is *Bomarea*. They are tuberous deciduous climbers closely related to *Alstroemeria* and like that genus their garden flowering season is from mid-summer until the first frosts. Most are rather tender, but a few from high altitude in Ecuador and Mexico seem to be reasonably hardy. Of these *Bomarea multiflora* JCA13761 collected by Jim and Jenny Archibald at 3200m in Ecuador has been most successful with us, even surviving into early January in 1998 when the flowers were powdered in snow. A week later temperatures of -4°C sent it into dormancy. The terminal clusters of 20 or more tubular flowers are green on the exterior and orange-scarlet inside, with prominent maroon spotting (variations on this theme are seen in most species). They are shown to their best when allowed to twine their way up through a large evergreen shrub such as a camellia from which they will emerge to look down at you. The flowers, targeted at hummingbirds, are also very popular with bees. For best results, feed and water them well during the growing season and protect the emergent shoots in the spring from slugs.

The most difficult group of shrubs and trees to associate bulbs with are the evergreens. The naturalised populations of *Rhododendron ponticum* in the British Isles illustrate the problem well: they let no light through so nothing will grow underneath. A problem that applies particularly to camellias is petal fall. Many varieties drop their flowers almost intact and these can smother the smaller early spring bulbs. One thing an evergreen provides that can aid the bulb grower is a 'wall' of foliage giving permanent shelter from sun or wind. Also its roots con-stantly draw moisture from the soil and this can be put to good use by the gardener. *Magnolia grandiflora* requires a sunny position to perform at its best, so a good specimen is likely to provide what is in effect a southerly aspect. Combined with its competitive root system, especially on heavier soils, this creates a habitat in which it may be possible to grow supposedly tender Californian and South African bulbs. Many *Calochortus* spp for instance like to grow in heavier substrates but really resent cold, wet maritime weather, although they are often temperature hardy. Because the roots of the evergreen draw out moisture throughout the year, the soil in its immediate vicinity tends not to become overly wet, and the evergreen foliage deflects some of the rainfall, giving an umbrella effect whilst also providing shelter from cold northerly winds. This helps reduce the risk of bulb rot in periods of cold, rainy winter weather. It also quickens the drying out of the soil in the summer, helping to give bulbs like *Calochortus* from a Mediterranean-type climate the summer rest they require. Using this idea with a leylandii conifer, I am now growing a surprising range of bulbs in a heavy clay soil. I can recommend *C. albus,* which grows about 25cm (10in) and has hanging globes of white or pink-blushed flowers, and *C. luteus,* which gets to about the same height but has deep yellow, upward-facing flowers, which show the chocolate blotch at the base of its petals. *Calochortus* are vulnerable to slugs! *Gladiolus trichonemifolius,* a winter-growing South African with grassy leaves and delicate-looking yellow flowers, which would never be recognised by Dame Edna, has also been successful in this situation. *Cyclamen graecum, C. libanoticum, C. mirabile* and *C.*

cyprium can all be grown in this way as can many other Mediterranean-type bulbs. It is also an appropriate site for trying such orchids as *Ophrys, Orchis* and *Pterostylis* spp.

I started by suggesting that bulbous plants had little to offer their shrubby companions. Using just the selection suggested above will create extra floral diversity in the garden and this of course means more invertebrates and birds too, leading to a more complicated garden ecology. In such an environment there should be lower pest invertebrate populations because there are more predators to deal with them. Good news for rhododendrons, magnolias and camellias!

References:

NORTH AMERICAN ROCK GARDEN SOCIETY, *Bulbs of North America*. Timber Press.

BRICKELL, Chistopher & SHARMAN, Fay. *The Vanishing Garden*. John Murray.

PRADHAN, Udai C. *Himalayan Cobra-lilies* (Arisaema) *Their Botany and Culture*. Primulaceae Books.

MATHEW, Brian. *The Smaller Bulbs*. Batsford.

CASE, Frederick W. Jr & Roberta B. *Trilliums*. Timber Press.

JACOBS, Don L. & Ron L. *American Treasures*. Eco Gardens

PHILLIPS, Roger & RIX, Martyn. *Bulbs*. Pan

FARRER. *The English Rock Garden*. Theophrastus.

GOLDBLATT, Peter & MANNING, John. *Gladiolus in Southern Africa*. Fernwood Press.

Kevin Hughes is a partner at Spinners Nursery, Boldre, Hampshire

GROUP TOUR TO DEVON

COMPILED BY VALERIE ARCHIBOLD

Fast Rabbit Farm (28 April 2002)

For those members who could not manage the main tour to Germany, Valerie Archibold provided a long weekend in Devon. We stayed again at the very comfortable Deer Park Hotel.

Fast Rabbit Farm was our first port of call. After a welcome coffee and biscuits we had a chance to walk around the nursery area where we found polytunnels stuffed with most desirable, often hard-to-find, rare plants (many of us left clutching at least one treasured pot), whilst outside were hardy shrubs including roses, camellias, magnolias and rhododendron, the latter including some large-leaved species of impressive size in tubs – a boon for the gardener in a hurry.

We were then ferried the short distance to the gardens, an extensive area created relatively recently out of water meadows and wooded hillside. Here we split into small groups to wander where our fancy took us – the pools and streamside or the wilder looking hillside – not forgetting a truly natural-looking rock garden near the entrance.

With loads of rhododendrons, magnolias and camellias there was too much to see in one visit – this is a garden I shall want to visit again. After lunch we drove to Black-pool Sands. This estate has been owned by the Newman family since about 1796, and has a small, sheltered beach and across a road and through a small wooden gate, a garden built up the steep hillside directly above the sea. Originally established in 1896, there are mature trees and shrubs – many rare and tender. The garden is being restored and reclaimed for the Newman family by Mr and Mrs Mort, the owners of Fast Rabbit Farm, and a fine job has so far been done. At present the ancient rhododendrons cannot be viewed as undergrowth and crumbling paths make them too much of an insurance risk, but there were many antipodean shrubs and other tender trees to admire and I think my most abiding memory is of huge cork oaks (*Quercus suber*) with trunks that have never been stripped of their corky bark, silvery and deeply fissured, and also of a collection of *Callistemon* spp, many I had never seen growing before. Think of all those borderline plants you would love to grow and that maybe you have under glass – here many of them are to be found growing and thriving all within a stones throw of the sea. Again I hope to return to see what more amazing plants will come to light as the restoration progresses.

Eileen Wheeler

Lukesland, Ivybridge (28 April 2002)

We were all delighted to have another chance to see this beautiful garden, which some members had to miss last year because of the foot and mouth epidemic. Mrs Rosemary Howell, owner of the garden with her husband Brian, very kindly gave us coffee on our arrival and led us on the tour of the garden. To read more about this remarkable garden a fuller account can be found in a copy of the 2001 Yearbook, compiled interestingly by our Secretary, Mrs Joey Warren.

Valerie Archibold

Woodland Grove, near Bovey Tracy (28 April 2002)

This garden is now owned by Peter and Helen Reynolds, and is spread over 21 acres with 11 of these planted out with rhododendrons, camellias and well-spaced trees, which form a light, sloping woodland. Some members will remember the beginning of this lovely garden when Peter's father, Major Dick Reynolds, began to plant rhododendrons and camellias with great enthusiasm many years ago. There are around 500 rhododendrons, and also a large number of camellias, which fringe the boundaries of the garden.

The Group was warmly welcomed and shown round by Peter. The property, once a bird sanctuary, has been in the family some 50 years. Rhododendrons are now the dominant plants, with the emphasis on the more showy hybrids, interspersed with many desirable species. Yellows are favourites here and include *R.* 'Crest', *R.* 'Odee Wright' and their offspring, the very floriferous *R.* 'Lila Pedigo', *R.* 'Cream Glory' *R.* 'Honey', *R.* 'Horizon', *R.* 'Monarch' and *R.* 'Idealist'. *R.* 'Loderi' is represented in many of its forms, including *R.* 'Princess Marina', *R.* 'Venus', *R.* 'Patience' *R.* 'Pink Topaz', *R.* 'Fairy Lace' and the rarely seen yellow form *R.* 'Julie'. Among the species are many less-common ones such as *R. lanatum* (the Sikkim form with the dark indumentum), *R.*

thayerianum, R. crinigerum, R. glischroides, R. neriiflorum, R. euchaites, R. fulvoides, R. piercei and especially a fine form form of *R. roxieanum* var. *oreonastes* having very long and very narrow leaves. There was a large and magnificently flowered plant of *R. johnstoneanum*. One more outstanding plant must be mentioned: *Camellia* 'Royalty', a superb *reticulata*.

Peter Reynolds propagates some of his treasures and kindly postponed his well-earned cup of tea to dig up a few plants from the nursery bed for those that had asked for them. This was a most enjoyable Sunday afternoon, sunny and pleasant despite the unsettled weather.

Stephen Fox

Sherwood (29 April 2002)

This well-labelled, exquisitely planted woodland garden, at Sir John and Lady Quicke's home, lies astride two small streams 10km (6 miles) west of Exeter. The 14 acres of acid clay lie at an elevation of 120m (400ft), and the annual rainfall is just under 75cm (30 in). Honey fungus is an unrelenting problem, and Sir John's policy has been to favour rhododendrons grafted on *R. ponticum* stock, in the belief that this stalwart has significant resistance to honey fungus; results largely confirm this.

Sherwood has the National Collection of Knaphill Azaleas, with over 100 cultivars, but the collection of *Magnolia* is even larger – 150 species and cultivars. First in the eastern valley were *M. campbellii* 'Darjeeling' (see back cover, bottom right), 'Elizabeth', 'Yellow Fever', 'Star Wars' and 'Judy' with its intriguing pointed buds; Sir John agrees with Jim Gardiner (*Rhododendrons with Camellias and Magnolias 2002*) in describing

'Star Wars' as one of the best tree magnolias in cultivation, but he has observed that the blooms of the newer magnolias may be small and poorly coloured in the first years of flowering. Rarely seen *M. rostrata* stood about 9m (30ft) but had only flowered once in 30 years. In the centre of the valley were *R. griffithianum* with those large, innocent white flowers and markedly pendent leaves, *R.* 'Catherine Fortescue' and one of the less-common Loderi Group, 'Loderi Julie', the 'yellowest' of the bunch. In the lap of the valley, a small pond was encased with *Rodgersia, Lysichiton,* and *Iris.* Nearby a rich red, evergreen azalea spilled onto the path, while wood anemones and lady's smocks flourished under Quicke policy not to mow before the end of May. A classical statue of the first Duke of Marlborough, a Quicke cousin, stood near *Magnolia* 'Vulcan', *M.* 'Susan', *M.* 'Yellow Bird' and another aristocrat, *M. sieboldii* subsp. *sinensis.*

By the house, Lady Prue's Herb Garden was bejewelled with some gorgeous tulips, *Tulipa saxatilis* and *T. acuminata,* while a stupendous *Stauntonia hexaphylla,* whose pendent clusters of fringed parchment flowers exhaled a rich perfume, thickly clothed one wall. Reaching the eaves on the next, a *Rosa banksiae* 'Lutea' and a *Fremontodendron californicum* prettily framed a bedroom window.

We emerged refreshed from the house to a lovely vista with red *Acer palmatum* centre stage. A huge *Rhododendron* 'Kewense' (nowadays sunk in the Loderi Group), 80 years old, was in full flower. Besides many mostly species rhododendrons, we saw a lovely specimen of *R.* 'Sarled', a unique yellow *Magnolia denudata,* obtained by Burncoose from China, which had flowered at 90cm (36in), and a delicious *R. pen-*

dulum 35 × 45cm (14 × 18in) in full flower. Sir John drew our attention to *Sambucus nigra* 'Black Beauty', which he described as a real stunner in June with its pink and white flowers set against the dark foliage. Down in the valley luxuriating species included a superb 4.5m (14ft) *R. falconeri.* The final stretch yielded more magnolias, *M. wilsonii,* a 15m (50ft) *M. campbellii* × *dawsoniana,* and the much admired Jury Hybrids 'Atlas' and 'Apollo'.

Hugh Dingle

Starveacre (29 April 2002)

After a wonderful morning at Sir John and Lady Quicke's garden at Sherwood, we returned for a buffet lunch at the Deer Park Hotel and then on to Starveacre for a relaxing afternoon.

The beauty and interest of the 4-acre garden lies in the diversity and often the rarity of its trees and rhododendrons. The garden was started nearly 20 years ago, at first a bare field sloping down, sometimes steeply, to an old woodland. In the first year or two, a hundred or more trees and shrubs were planted, and more were gradually added over the following years. About half of the trees are coniferous and most were donated by Humphrey Welch, a leading authority on conifers. Humphrey moved down to Dorset when he retired from his dwarf conifer nursery and took more plants with him than he could accommodate in his new garden. So we were lucky recipients of many of his conifers.

But a rare conifer, once called *Pilgerodendron uviferum* and now called *Librocedrus uvifera,* was given to us by Ambrose Congreve when we were visiting Ireland. There are only a few in this country, and it is growing well.

An area of woodland on the south side of the garden is planted out with species rhododendrons, including such rarities as *R. lanigerum* CC 7526, *R. anthosphaerum*, *R. sikangense* var. *exquisitum* CNW 924, *R. cynocarpum* KR 4051A, *R. tsariense* 'Yum Yum', *R. principis* KR 3084 and many others, mainly grown from wild-collected seed from China and Tibet.

At the north end of the garden is another collection of species rhododendrons, sheltered from the east by the hills above and also by a high covering of oak trees. Many were in flower at the time of our visit including *R.* 'Chrysomanicum', a lovely deep yellow cross between *R. burmanicum* and *R. chrysodoron*. The Group gave one of these to Sir John Quicke that morning as a 'thank you' for our visit to Sherwood. Other plants in flower in this long bed were *R. megacalyx*, *R. ambiguum*, *R. xanthocodon*, and *R. valentinianum*, two yellow and two white.

Fringing this bed is a collection of tender rhododendrons, such as *R.* 'Countess of Sefton', *R. camelliiflorum*, *R. dendricola*, all giving off a delightful scent, and mostly in shades of cream or white.

Members could walk down from these collections, past the swimming pool (fringed with rhododendrons and other shrubs) and along meandering paths, flanked by acers, conifers and rhododendrons, and enjoy the quietness before walking up for tea in the conservatory, and the end of a most enjoyable tour.

Valerie Archibold

GROUP TOUR TO NORTH GERMANY

OVERVIEW

In times past country folk near the North Sea coast of Germany often ate with a single spoon. From this same spoon they also drank their schnapps.

> Ick seh di – Dat freit mi!
> Ick sup di to – Dat do
> Prost!

Roughly translated from the Low German dialect of northern Germany:

> I see you – I'm glad of that!
> I drink to you – Do that
> Cheers!

This is the opening exchange of a ritual toast with which guests in the Oldenburg region are welcomed. The toast is made with the traditional tin spoon brimming with schnapps and held in the left hand.

Oldenburg, west of Bremen, was our base for the tour and our welcome by Hans-Dieter Bruns at our first garden, the Bruns Rhododendron Park, included this traditional 'spoon drink', after glasses of excellent German beer. Our welcome was thus warm in every sense; and it set the tone perfectly for what was to come throughout the tour – a feast of rhododendrons made the more enjoyable by the warmth of the welcome from the hosts.

The pattern was established: from this first visit – Bruns Park, a 10 hectare woodland with free public access, comprising some 800 rhododendron taxa under a pine topcover with a secondary storey of acers, cornus, hamamelis, magnolias etc, plus our beer and schnapps – to our last visit – Teufelsmoor, the small, private garden of Katharina Haunschild and Hans Bergeman. This was by contrast a very personal creation made on an 8m (25ft) depth of moss peat, with the plantings drifting out naturalistically into the wild moor – and followed by a palatial spread of food and drink in ancient farm buildings, surrounded by old farming memorabilia.

Our party numbered 18, four from Russia, two from the USA and twelve from across the UK. The enthusiasm of our group matched that of our hosts in showing us their collections, and the language of the plants made good any potential deficiencies in verbal communication.

The following accounts of individual garden and nursery visits by four members of the party reflect in different ways the range of experiences we enjoyed and I hope will convey a sense of the pleasures such tours can bring, on many levels.

Our special thanks are due to Valerie Archibold for her hard work in organising all the detail of a balanced and busy itinerary; to Moswins Tours for their excellent package of accommodation and travel arrangements and to our German friends for the warmth of their welcome and their generosity and hospitality throughout.

Nurseries and gardens visited:
  Bruns Rhododendron Park
  Hobbie Rhododendron Waldpark
  Maxwald Park
  Teufelsmoor
  Hachmann Nursery
  Schlossgarten, Oldenburg
  Bremen Rhododendron Park
  Forderkreis Arboretum
  Landwirtschaftskammer Weser-Ems
Maurice Foster

Bruns Rhododendron Park (25 May 2002)
This was the first visit of our tour where we were made welcome by the proprietor, Herr Hans-Dieter Bruns, who was with us for the whole of the tour.

We soon learned that the dominant feature of all the rhododendron gardens was the German climate, which was very kind to us while we were there, but it can give rise to early morning frosts at any time in the year. This leads to a concentration on the hybrids of the more hardy species, effectively to the exclusion of all else. There is a relatively narrow season, unlike that of the benign climate of the west coast of England, and it is really confined from late May into June and is for hybrids themselves being derived from relatively few species. The parentage of the plants in this aspect is so critical that in the catalogues the plants are listed more by their parentage than any other factor.

We were introduced to a development in the growth of rhododendrons, which is assuming a very high profile in the major nurseries, and that is of grafting on to root stock that is alkaline tolerant. The specific rootstock known by the registered trade mark of "Inkarho", which I understand is a cross between 'Cunningham's White' and *R. fortunei*, but that is hearsay rather than established fact. The major growers in Germany have banded together and established "Inkarho" as a registered trade mark registered under stock and are exploiting it commercially.

John Harsant

Landwirtschaftskammer Wester-Ems (25 May 2002)
This visit was to a research station and also a horticultural show, which, to all intents and purposes, appeared to be one establishment with two functions: horticultural research and public display.

This is a major project that clearly demonstrates the great interest in horticulture amongst the German public today, and it is a most interesting exposition. The horticultural show itself is a little reminiscent of a garden festival and contains a large number of beds, which, apart from some scientific interest, are used for growing on many plants that will be used to restock the older established garden of the research station.

We were shown a number of trials of plants growing in soils of various pH: some grafted onto 'Cunningham's White' and others on "Inkarho". There was indeed a significant improvement where the pH was 6.5 or higher but at typical UK levels there was no apparent improvement in performance by those plants grafted onto "Inkarho".

One feature that emerged from this was that in Germany far better performance is generally achieved by grafting rather than by growing hybrids on their own roots.

John Harsant

Das Arboretum Forderkreis Ellerhoop-Thiensen (26 May 2002)

We made an early start for the 2½-hour drive to the Ellerhoop-Thiensen Arboretum, northwest of Hamburg. The original arboretum was established on the site in 1956, and was extended to 17 hectares in 1980, when it was acquired by the local council. In 1996, when it was threatened with closure, it was taken over by the Friends of the Arboretum, who are now responsible for its management.

Shortly after entering the arboretum the visitor encounters a display of the development of trees from the carbon age (about 400 million years ago) to the present day. In this area we saw a rare specimen of *Asimina triloba* and a *Magnolia hypoleuca*.

In the centre of the arboretum is a charmingly designed water landscape, with islands and flooded locations, which is used to study the anatomic adaptation of plants to the environment. Around this area were planted various hydrophytic tree types such as *Acer rubrum, Aronia arbutifolia, Cephalanthus occidentalis, Ilex glabra, Nyssa aquatica* and *Taxodium distichum*.

Another focal area for research is the breeding and selection of tree peonies. Over the years, the arboretum has accumulated the largest collection in Germany, including 245 species. A particular study has been made of *Paeonia rockii,* and its hybrids; the arboretum contains some 500 specimens.

Other features of the arboretum include a cottage garden, a section for rare native plants and shrubs, and a collection of the main crops grown in the world. The arboretum provides interest for the casual visitor, material for the scientist and education for students of all ages.

Martin Gates

Hachmann's Nursery at Barmstedt (26 May 2002)

The Group was welcomed and shown around by Holger Hachmann, who has now assumed responsibility for the running of this large and important family business. However, we also had the opportunity of meeting Holger's father, Hans Hachmann, who founded the nursery and is still very active; since 1989 he has bred and raised over 3,000 varieties although only a minority of them have gone into production. Hardiness, resistance to disease and ease of propagation are important factors in the selection of hybrids, apart from the obvious considerations of beauty, flowering season, novelty and fashion, which translate into customer demand. A large part of the nursery is given over to the display garden, which contains a huge assortment of every possible type of hardy rhododendron.

The 2002 Yearbook contained an account of some of Hachmann's best-known hybrids and these were on view in the garden, along with many others still on trial or destined not to go into production. Each year a selection of 20 to 60 is made out of a crop of 25,000 seedlings. A name is given to each selection. Of these only three to ten find their way into the catalogue. It is interesting to note that, unlike some other nurseries in Germany, Hachmanns avoid the use of *R. smirnowii* as a breeding parent as they have found it susceptible to leaf spot.

Hachmanns graft all their elepidote rhododendrons as they believe that an understock of 'Cunningham's White' or (for high-pH soils only) "Inkarho" confers a longer life; care is therefore taken to avoid scion-rooting. The understock is given a long, diagonal slice just above soil level and mated with a similarly sliced scion, the union being secured with grafting tape. (In Germany, this type of side-grafting is given the strange name of "kopulation"). Propagation experts can manage up to 100 grafts per hour. The grafts are planted about 25cm (10in) apart in trays containing peat and housed in a greenhouse of controlled temperature and humidity until the autumn. They are then transferred to peat moss with a little chalk in 13cm (5in) pots and stood in the open until the following year, when they are planted in open ground and grown on for another year (using some liquid fertiliser) before being sold.

Azaleas are rooted with hormone but the Japanese sorts do not require this.

Among the uncatalogued plants two should be mentioned: 'Glühlicht', a dazzlingly intense orange azalea, and 'Filegran', a cross between *R. roxieanum* and 'Graziella', a diminutive, narrow-leaved and floriferous form of *R. ponticum*.

Stephen Fox

Hobbie's Rhododendron Park at Westerstede (27 May 2002)

The name of Dietrich Hobbie has long been familiar to rhododendron enthusiasts in Britain owing to the popularity of his *R. forrestii* crosses such as 'Gertrude Schale' and 'Elizabeth Hobbie'. These and other Hobbie Hybrids were the subject of an article by Slocock in the 1966 Yearbook. We were therefore delighted to discover that our hostess and guide for the morning was none other than Elizabeth Hobbie herself, the daughter of Dietrich, who died in 1985.

Our schedule did not give us time to visit to the large Hobbie nursery, only the associated Rhododendron Park, which extends to 70 hectares, and in a corner of which is Elizabeth's superbly located home. The Park was started in 1929 by Dietrich Hobbie, on woodland that had been in the family for some centuries The land is only 10m (30ft) above sea level and is rich in forest litter. Hobbie obtained plants and collectors' seed from England during the 1930s but soon discovered that many of the species he admired were too tender for him to grow in the wood. He embarked on a programme of hybridisation to overcome this problem, starting in 1939.

The Park contains most of the 70 species that are listed in the catalogue and which were the principal material used by Dietrich Hobbie for his crosses. His favourite species were *R. forrestii* (15 hybrids currently listed) and *R. williamsianum* (11 hybrids). He also used *R. catawbiense, R. brachycarpum, R. insigne* and, latterly, *R. yakushimanum*. The tradition has been carried on by Elizabeth Hobbie, one of whose hybrids, 'Maisonne' (*R. yakushimanum* × 'Britannia') has white indumented leaves and flowers rose-pink outside and white inside the corolla – with characteristic modesty, Elizabeth attributes this cross to her father.

Among the many impressive rhododendron plants we saw were 'Nymphenberg' (a *R. discolor* × *decorum* hybrid, white with yellow markings and scented), 'Gartendirector Rieger' ('Adriaan Koster' × *R. williamsianum*, cream with red markings) and 'Ehrengold' (a *R. wardii* hybrid with long-lasting flowers of gold, pink in the bud).

The Park is much more than an assembly of rhododendrons. Its structure depends on the skillful planting of pines and exotic conifers such as *Picea omorika, Cunninghamia lanceolata* and *Metasequoia*.

Stephen Fox

Maxwald Park (27 May 2002)

Following our most enjoyable visit to the Hobbie Rhododendron Park, we visited the privately owned Maxwald Park and garden, which is nearby.

Maxwald Park comprises 10 hectares of natural woodland, planted with rhododendrons and other trees and shrubs, together with more formal gardens around the house. We were shown around by Dr Eberhard Pühl, who is the great grandson of G D Bohlje, who created the rhododendron woodland between 1888 and 1912; subsequently Dr Pühl's mother added various conifers to the existing planting. We were accompanied by Walter Schmalscheidt, a local rhododendron expert.

The woodland contained numerous *R. ponticum* and 'Catawbiense Grandiflorum', but the most interesting plants were the old Waterer and Ghent hybrids, which included 'Frederick Waterer', 'Ignatius Sargent', 'James Marshall Brookes', 'Leopardi', 'Purpureum Elegans', 'Stella Waterer' and 'Ignis Nova'.

Among the trees we noted *Abies grandis, Pinus rigida* and *Picea omorika*. In the garden around the house we saw *Betula nana, Magnolia sieboldii* and an old rose 'Stanmore Perpetual'. There is an English yew garden with topiary in the manner of Great Dixter and a small area in the style of Gertrude Jekyll, surrounded by a lime walk.

After viewing the garden we were invited into the house for refreshments by Dr Pühl, who had been delighted to show us his park and garden.

Martin Gates

The Rhododendron Park and Botanic Garden, Bremen (28 May 2002)

Frau Julia Westhoff, Director of the Rhododendron Park and the Botanic Garden, was our guide, and she introduced Berndt-Adolf Crome, President of The German Rhododendron Society. Frau Anna Scheer also joined us here.

The statue of a bison commemorates the Park's origin in 1888 as a merchant's hunting estate. In 1936, The German Rhododendron Society was given this land by the city of Bremen to become their headquarters. The soil pH is 3.7–5.5. *R. catawbiense* seedlings were planted here in 1936, in the oldest part of the Park.

Julia's predecessor, Dr Heft, had laid out the paths and areas, and planted companion plants such as *Pieris*, to flower before, and *Kalmia*, to flower after the rhododendrons; she is planting hydrangeas, to follow on with colour in August/September.

The German hybrids from Georg Arends were planted in the 1950s, and Japanese Azaleas planted in the 1960s were given names of rivers, alphabetically. 170 varieties of Mortier Ghent hybrids, hardy hybrids of the 1830s, provide a glorious display of scent and colour. Tall trees among the plantings give shade, and majesty to the stands of big, old rhododendron hybrids.

The most common query is about pruning rhododendrons, so Julia has created a small area showing rhododendron bushes cut hard down, showing their regeneration at two, three, four and five years' growth. A beautiful *R. yakushimanum* FCC form, perhaps 60 years old, was splendid against a holly tree. 'Helene Schiffner' FCC form is the whitest of whites, and grows much more compactly in Germany than in England.

A collection of Hachmann hybrids, early and late flowerers, were planted together twelve years ago; a collection of *R. yakushimanum* hybrids has been planted more recently in the new part of the Botanic Garden. Hardy species (including a few Lepidotes) are planted in the rock garden with Japanese Azaleas and planted alphabetically.

The Botanical Garden was created in 1935 from an older garden. Between 1950 and 1960, plantings were made, separated into continents, together with beds of native plants. Here, too, are samples of balcony boxes, for bright colour; medical and herb gardens; a large carpet-bedding display of a sundial; and the heather garden is vast 'lawn' of *Calluna vulgaris*.

Julia is seeking 50- to 100-year-old hardy hybrids from the famous nurseries, and asked the Rhododendron Group of the RHS to help.

Joey Warren

Teufelsmoor – Frau Haunschild (28 May 2002)

Prof. Dr W. Spethmann from the Institute of Horticulture, Hannover University, joined us here.

Frau Haunschild led us into her 180-year-old farmhouse for refreshments, and to see how people in Germany lived in those days, as it is kept, and used, as originally built and furnished.

This 'different' garden is very low lying and we walked on springy turf and moss through open birch, oak and pine woodland dotted with rhododendrons. Past a romantic summerhouse, placed on a slight rise for a view, the garden slopes gradually down to natural marsh and pools of water, with birch trees, moss, even bog cotton, pine trees, and vacciniums. The garden was a peat moss working; it is now regenerating and is a natural area. Frau Haunschild has gardened here for many years, overcoming opposition,

and it is now an established conservation garden and a wildlife haven.

After a magnificent tea, we raced back to Oldenburg.

Joey Warren

Schlossgarten, Oldenburg (28 May 2002)

We are grateful to Dr Erhard Pühl, who recommended that we should add this garden to our itinerary, where the very first, oldest rhododendrons in Germany grow. He met us at the castle entrance to show us the garden. The castle was built in 1818, and the rhododendrons were planted there in 1828 for the Duke of Oldenbourg. After 1918, the castle and garden in Oldenbourg became civic property.

The magnificent trees included *Fagus sylvatica* var. *heterophylla* (fern-leaved beech), *Ostrya carpinifolia* (hop hornbeam), *Sequoiadendron giganteum* (wellingtonia), *Tilia cordata* (small-leaved lime) 1814, *Quercus robur* (common/English oak) at least 300 years old, conifers planted in 1865, *Ptercarya fraxinifolia* (wingnut), and a stand of four huge *Liriodendron tulipfera* (tulip tree) (there had been eight originally, but a disastrous storm in 1922 felled the other four). English rhododendrons were planted in 1885; Herr Schmallacheit had identified most of them already, so some were named, for example 'Mrs T.H. Lowinsky' and 'Chionoides'. We could only suggest some names, or possible parents for those planted in 1828 (*R. catawbiense, R. ponticum, R. caucasicum, R. grandiflorum, R. fortunei*).

The English Rhododendron Walk was planted in 1885 with plants from Waterers Nursery, including 'Duke of York' and 'John Waterer'.

Joey Warren

OBITUARY

Dr James Ambler Smart MBE, VMH

Jimmy died in his chair, well-deserved whisky glass in hand, at the end of a day that included a morning spent in the potting shed, helping to pot plants for his beloved garden. He was active to the end, despite losing some mobility, helped by what some of us called his "speed-mobile" which enabled him to tackle all but the steepest paths in his garden.

Jimmy's interest in gardening appears to have started when he was a medical student at St Thomas' Hospital in London. He developed an Alpine House in the family garden at Warlingham, Surrey where he housed his collection of plants from European sources.

He qualified as a doctor in 1937 and in 1939 joined the RNVR to work as a ship's doctor. He had a dangerous war, being in three ships that were hit either by magnetic mines, bombed or torpedoed, before being awarded the MBE for his acts of bravery when HMS Hermes was sunk in the Bay of Bengal in April 1942; the only decoration made to the ship's company. He was a Surgeon Lieutenant Commander at the time, and gained his award for swimming in the oily water treating the injured and comforting the dying. The canvas wallet he wore round his chest, which he had made as a result of his previous shipwrecks, contained water, syringe and morphine, all of which proved invaluable in the water. These were the actions of a brave and very practical man.

In 1946 he returned to civilian life to study and became a GP and anaesthetist with the famous Bear Street practice in Barnstaple, North Devon, later dropping the GP to become a full-time anaesthetist at the North Devon Infirmary until the late 1970s. He moved to Marwood in 1949, with his sister and her son, John, moving into the present house in 1966. He could see the potential for creating a fabulous garden at Marwood from the time of his initial move to the village, and, despite being a busy doctor, made a start. In November 1966 he made contact with my father, David Trehane, who was starting to collect camellia varieties and develop his nursery. Jimmy bought 12in plants of 'Ville de Nantes' and 'Bow Bells' for £1.5.0 each and one of 'Phil Doak' for £3.3.0, plus a blueberry, which he stressed he wanted for its "leaf colour and flower". This was the beginning of a long and mutually beneficial friendship between these two dedicated plantsmen, but it was not until early 1969 that the two men started communicating on Christian-name terms. How times have changed!

Following a debilitating illness in 1967, Jimmy spent his convalescence visiting a great many camellia places in the US, exchanged many letters with my father and warned of the prevalence of camellia flower blight and the dangers of importing plants with flower buds, from infected areas.

He sent many packets of scions to David for rooting or grafting and the resulting plants were later shared between them. Rhododendrons and magnolias began to appear in the correspondence too, and many other plants were gradually included. Both men took many transparencies and exchanged these too.

On his return, in April 1968, Jimmy's garden became an important focus for his leisure time, with the construction of his camellia display house and the excavation of the valley floor to create the first two lakes. The walled garden was dedicated to his camellia collection. He even tried using gibberellic acid, with limited success, in the American manner, to promote earliness and large blooms.

Malcolm Pharoah joined him as head gardener in 1970 and the most rapid development of the garden really began from this time. This did not stop Jimmy's travels. He visited New Zealand and made friends with the Jury family, famous for their camellia and magnolia breeding, and sent back scions from them and other sources in both countries. He regularly spent time with his nephew, John and his family in Australia, particularly after his retirement in the mid 1970s, always returning to England with suitcases full of plants, leaving shoes and clothes behind to make room for them!

Jimmy always maintained that to be a "one-genus enthusiast" was not a good thing and his knowledge and interest encompassed many genera, from trees to small bulbs and alpines. He was a great collector. The garden extended up the hill on the other side of the stream below the house, and Marwood's National Collection of *Astilbe* by the lake below it joined the National Collections of *Iris ensata* and *Tulbaghia*.

Rhododendrons do not stand out as a special feature at Marwood, but his collection of cultivars and species were chosen because he liked them. His magnolia collection was a source of pride and joy, and it was fitting that the magnolias were particularly magnificent in Jimmy's last month including 'Marwood Spring', named by Jimmy.

Jimmy was a valued member of the RHS Rhododendron and Camellia Committee from 1982 to 1996, and camellias from Marwood featured regularly at meetings, with many gaining AMs or FCCs. He was always generous with material from his plants, provided visitors had a genuine interest in them. With his collection of around 1,000 different camellia cultivars in the garden and his knowledge of the provenance of them, he did much to increase both knowledge and enjoyment of camellias. He was a worthy first recipient of the RHS David Trehane Cup, in 2000, awarded for just these sort of contributions.

In 1994 he had a "bumper" year, celebrating his 80th birthday, being awarded the VMH by the RHS and relinquishing his bachelor days by marrying Margaret. Together they shared their interest in gardening and spent the next few years making whirlwind tours visiting friends, acquaintances and plant places in Europe, South Africa, Australia, New Zealand and America.

Back home, the garden provided Jimmy with a focus right to the end, with Margaret to share it and to provide the loving support he needed in his final years. Fortunately the garden is in safe hands, under the ownership of Jimmy's nephew, John Snowdon, and the management of Malcolm Pharoah and his team of dedicated gardeners.

The garden is Jimmy's memorial and it is fitting that a splendid statue of him stands in the valley below the house. It somehow conveys the mixture of serious academic ability with the wit and above all the enthusiasm of the man.

A special event, probably at Marwood, is to be organised in 2004, when John Snowdon and all his family will be free to travel from Australia, to celebrate and honour Jimmy Smart's life. It is hoped to launch a scholarship or award for gardeners, with a link to rhododendrons and camellias.

Jennifer Trehane

COMPETITIONS

**Early Rhododendron Competition
12–13 March 2002**

I have been very fortunate to take over reporting the Early Competition from David Farnes in such a good year for early flower, and should like to begin by paying tribute to the painstaking and excellent reports he produced over the years – some of those years very lean indeed.

So what were my first impressions of this year's displays? To start with two small grumbles: my initial concern on entering the hall was that no rhododendrons were to be seen, and, after finding them tucked away into a far corner, that there was not enough bench space – an observation confirmed by one of the major exhibitors who had had to leave many of the plants, so laboriously prepared, in his van.

But what a glorious sea of yellow met the eye! – enough to clothe the most fastidious Chinese emperor – though he might not have appreciated that most of the colour was contributed by the plants of northeast India. *R. macabeanum* and its progeny were everywhere – and the journey to London was made well worthwhile for this alone.

As well as familiar exhibits like *R. irroratum* 'Polka Dot' and the Exbury *R. calophytum*, some exceptional and unusual forms of species stick in my mind: the *R. macabeanum* from Tregothnan, a good yellow with four "layers" of flowers building up the truss, and their outstanding yellow *R. glaucophyllum* (or should it be *R. luteiflorum*?); the *R. arboreum album* from Exbury; *R. pocophorum* from Hergest Croft; and the *R. sherriffii* from Hilliers. Such outstanding forms deserve to be made widely known.

The twelve species classes attracted a total of 86 entries, with five exhibitors having gardens ranging from two to hundreds of acres achieving first or second places.

Class 1, for three species, was won by Exbury with a pale *R. macabeanum*, their outstanding *R. calophytum* with red pedicels, and a good large truss of *R. barbatum*. Placing Clyne second with a good *R. macabeanum*, *R. argipeplum* and a spotted *R. irroratum*, must have taken the judges some time. Hergest Croft had the best *R. macabeanum* with a deeper colour but could only manage third.

Class 2, for a species spray or truss, had one of the most remarkable sprays I have ever seen: three trusses of *R. macabeanum* from Tregothnan wonderfully presented. The second – six trusses on a spray of *R. irroratum* 'Polka Dot' would have won most prizes most years, and there was a first class *R. macabeanum* from Exbury – unfortunately slightly marked. *R. racemosum* from Exbury was rightly highly commended. All 16 entries were of very high quality.

Class 3, for one truss of a species, had 14 entries. First was a magnificent *R. macabeanum* from Exbury, with *R. sutchuenense* of an excellent colour from Hergest Croft a close second, and *R. beanianum* from Hilliers was an unusual and welcome third. *R. macabeanum* from Clyne this time was highly commended.

Class 4, for one truss of a species in subsects Arborea or Argyrophylla, gave Exbury first of eight entries with a beautifully presented *R. arboreum album*. *R. roseum* took second and third places for the Hillier Arboretum (Hilliers) and Clyne.

Class 5, for a truss from subsects Barbata, Glischra or Maculifera, was won by Tregothnan with a *R. glischroides* that had collapsed a little by Tuesday lunch time. A *R. argipeplum* from Clyne showed a very nice contrast between flower and foliage and took second.

Class 6, for a truss of a species from subsects Falconera and Grandia, had *R. macabeanum* first, second and third. Clyne's paler truss was preferred to Brian Wright's good yellow and Exbury's cream. Brian's truss labelled *R. giganteum* with cream flowers and grey indumentum grown at 200m (600ft) in Sussex was of high quality and great interest and should attract the attention of the taxonomists.

Class 7, for a truss from subsect. Fortunea. Only four entries, and won by Exbury with their excellent *R. calophytum*. A rather open truss of *R. sutchuenense* from Clyne was second, with *R. oreodoxa* from Hilliers a good third.

Class 8, for a spray from subsect. Neriiflora, brought Hilliers a good first with *R. sperabile* var. *weihsiense*, and second also with a lovely *R. catacosmum* with its drooping pink bells. Clyne's bright *R. neriiflorum* was placed third, but an excellent *R. pocophorum* from Hergest Croft was unplaced.

Class 9, for a truss from subsects Campylocarpa, Thomsonia, Selensia or Williamiana, won by a welcome stranger from Hilliers – a delightful, plum-coloured *R. sherriffii* with its wonderful foliage. The only other entry was a very good second for *R. eclecteum* from Brian Wright.

Class 10, for a Lepidote spray, had nine good entries. Hilliers were placed ahead of Brian Wright's excellent *R. lutescens* with their *R. racemosum* 'Rock Rose' just opening, and there was a glorious yellow *R. glaucophyllum* from Tregothnan, which was only third.

Class 11, for any other species, saw another first for the perfectly shaped truss of *R.*

irroratum 'Polka Dot' from Exbury, and second also to them with *R. fulvum*. A lovely pink *R. principis* with nice foliage gave Hillier's third, and it was nice to see a perfect *R. tanastylum* at the show from Clyne (see Fig. 27) – the flower deserving a higher placing, perhaps, but the exhibit did not sit well in its vase.

Class 12, for a spray from any other species, gave Hilliers a first for their *R. principis*, with Exbury getting third with *R. fulvum*. Second went to a colourful *R. keysii* from Tregothnan.

The hybrid section attracted 40 entries with five exhibitors taking first or second places. Exbury and Clyne did extremely well, but once again placings were achieved by competitors with smaller gardens.

The first prizes in classes 13 to 18 and 20 to 21 respectively were won by Exbury, Clyne, High Beeches, Clyne, Exbury, Clyne, Chris Fairweather and, again, Chris Fairweather.

There were many outstanding hybrids on show, many well known both on the show bench and in the garden. I hope that someone's enterprise and generosity will soon result in some of the more unusual taxa (singled out below) being listed in the *RHS Plant Finder*.

'Edgar Stead' (part of Exbury's winning entry for class 13) is a superlative red with a perfect truss. It is a hybrid containing *R. zeylanicum*, *R. thomsonii* and *R. barbatum* and, if hardy, should be on everyone's wish list; it is like *R. barbatum* but with much bigger flowers. Exbury's 'Scheherezade' clone of Nimrod in classes 13 and, I think, 17, with its picotee pink was also mouth watering – but unfortunately not easily available. Classes 13 and 16 also contained another really good and unknown vibrant red with nice spotting and startling black nectar pouches – *R. barbatum* × *elliottii* KW 19083 from Hillier's – part of their third prize. Finally the winner for Clyne in class 16 – the Medea grex – 'Red Admiral' × *R. sutchuenense* (also part of their second prize in class 13) is well worthy of notice.

'Florida Ogada' – a Hope Finlay cross *R. macabeanum* × *sinogrande* shown by High Beeches was rightly given the FCC at the show and was the winner of class 15. The truss is enormous by even Scottish standards and the plant is grown in the drier atmosphere of Sussex. There are probably other big-leaf hybrids lurking in gardens and I hope members will be encouraged to show them after the success of this one. It is a wonderful plant, which we hope will be propagated. The unusual *R. chrysomanicum*, with its deep golden glow in the throat was unplaced in the same class in the face of excellent 'Ibex' (*R. griersoninum* × *pocophorum*) (also second in class 15) – a fine pink from Hilliers, and a *R. hodgsonii* cross from Clyne.

A spray of 'Fire Prince' ('Britannia' × *R. arboreum* subsp. *delavayi*) from Exbury, erroneously labelled 'Fire Dance', was placed second in class 14, behind the well-known and beautifully poised 'Emasculum' from Clyne. 'Fire Prince' has very bright red *R. arboreum*-type flowers with white stamens. Please can I have one? Also worthy of attention was the 'Werei' (*R. arboreum* × *barbatum*) – an old hybrid from Penjerrick (AM 1921) shown by Exbury and placed second in class 16 – an unusual pink with *R. arboreum*-type foliage.

There was a really nice *R. calophytum* hybrid from Clyne with a subtle blotch and good foliage placed third in class 17, and the same stable showed a grande hybrid of a lovely shade of cream in class 18 (second to their own hodgsonii hybrid). Surely these crosses are worth naming and registering?

Chris Fairweather's Vireyas dominated classes 20 and 21. What an excellent job he is doing in popularising this largest section of the *Rhododendron* family, with the first prize winners 'Ne Plus Ultra' and 'First Light', as well as others surely being taxa that will "sell on sight" to both specialists and house plant enthusiasts.

Finally, mention must be made of the *Magnolia* class, especially when there are considerable difficulties in getting exhibits to stay fresh on their journeys from far flung parts of the country. The spray of *M. dawsoniana* 'Chyverton', which won the class, was beautifully poised – all the flowers in near perfect condition, but paler than is usual with this cultivar. Second was a wonderfully coloured pink (as pure a colour as 'Star Wars') from Tregothnan labelled *M. campbellii* – superbly held flowers but feeling the journey a little, and the *M. mollicomata* subsp. *lanarth* from the same stable was its usual striking self but drooping distinctly. Tregothnan also got fourth with a 'Star Wars' just opening. 'Merrill' from Ann Hooton, and 'Leonard Messel' from Chyverton were also very attractive, as was 'Treve Holman', which was going over.

It was also very nice to see a good vase of *Michelia doltsopa* (now we are told, a magnolia) in Class 2. Congratulations to all those showing magnoliaceae so well. Let's hope to see more in the future.

Mike Robinson

Main Rhododendron Competition – Species 23–24 April 2002

Once again it is sad to report that there were so few exhibitors at this show, especially in a year when the weather had been kind for exhibitors.

On a brighter note, I felt that the quality of the exhibits were better than last year, which gave many visitors to the show great pleasure – very evident by the numerous questions and favourable comments I received.

Of great interest was *R. wightii* shown by Dr Jack from Scotland. Confirmed by Dr Chamberlain as the true species, it was quite different from the familiar form, pale yellow in colour, having a smaller truss and not lax in habit. Possibly a Hooker introduction.

Class 1, six species, one truss of each, The Lionel de Rothschild Challenge Cup. First Prize to Exbury Garden with *R. fictolacteum, R. degronianum* subsp. *heptamerum, R. falconeri, R. arizelum, R. rubiginosum,* and *R. niveum.*

Class 2, three species, one truss of each. First prize awarded to Exbury Garden for showing a rather deep-coloured *R. orbiculare, R. irroratum, R. anhweiense,* took the judges eye, closely followed in second place by B.E. Wright of Crowborough with *R. aberconwayi, R. arboreum* and *R. orbiculare.*

Class 3, any species, one truss, The McLaren Challenge Cup. A near-perfect *R. niveum* from the Isabella Plantation, Richmond Park took first prize. Second prize went to *R. roxieanum* var. *orionastes* from Dr Jack. Third prize to B.E. Wright's *R. aberconwayi.*

Class 4, any species, one spray not exceeding 75cm (30in) in height from the top of vase, The Rosa Stevenson Challenge Cup. Only two entries. A well-staged, superb vase of *R. searsiae* from Exbury won the Challenge Cup. Second went to Anne Hooton from Lowood, West Sussex with a vase of 'Ken Janeck' (one of a number of good exhibits staged for the first time for a number of years).

Class 5, any species of subsects Arborea or Argyrophylla, one truss. The same two exhibitors as in class 4 competed again here with Exbury's *R. niveum* just in front of Anne Hooton's *R. argyrophyllum* 'Chinese Silver'.

Class 6, any species of subsects Barbata, Glischra or Maculifera, one truss. A fine *R. anhweiense* from Exbury was the winner. Dr

Jack's *R. adenosum* gained the second prize (no mean achievement to stage an exhibit in such good form after air travel from Scotland). B.E. Wright was in third place with *R. anhweiense.*

Class 7, any species of subsects Campanulata, Fulgensia or Lanata, one truss. The only entry was *R. campanulatum* from Dr Jack, and was awarded a third prize.

Class 8, any species of subsects Grandia or Falconera, one truss. Exbury Garden were awarded first and second prize with a good, clean *R. rex* subsp. *fictolacteum* and *R. macabianum* – the latter rather small.

Class 9. Any species of subsect. Fortunea, one truss. Exbury just beat B.E. Wright, both exhibiting *R. orbiculare.*

Class 10, any species of subsects Fulva, Irrorata or Parishia, one truss. In this class B.E. Wright turned the table, beating Exbury's *R. irroratum* with his *R. aberconwayi.*

Class 11, and species of subsect. Taliensia, one truss. A very pretty *R. roxieanum* var. *oreonastes* shown by Dr Jack just pipped B.E. Wright's *R. bureavii.*

Class 12, any species of subsect. Neriiflora, one spray not exceeding 30cm (12in) in height from the top of the vase. The only entry from Exbury of *R. neriiflorum* was worthy of first prize.

Class 13, any species of subsect. Pontica, one truss. Exbury were first with their *R. degronianum* subsp. *heptamerum.* Dr Jack came second with *R. caucasicum,* and Anne Hooton was third with *R. hyperythrum.*

Class 14, any species of subsects Thomsonia, Selensia or Campylocarpa, one spray not exceeding 30cm (12in) in height from the top of the vase. The only entry from Exbury of *R. campylocarpum* was awarded first prize.

Class 15, one spray of *R. williamsianum,* one spray not exceeding 30cm (12in) in height from the top of the vase. *R. williamsianum* from Exbury, the only entry, gained first prize.

Class 18, any species of subsects Maddenia ("Dalhousiae Alliance" and "Megacalyx Alliance" only), one truss, grown in the open or otherwise. Exbury provided the only two entries: a charming *R. burmanicum* was placed first with *R. parryae* second.

Class 19, any species of subsects Triflora or Heliolepida other than *R. augustinii*, one spray not exceeding 45cm (18in) in height from top of the vase. *R. searsiae* from Exbury gained first prize. B.E. Wright's lovely clean, in both flower and foliage, *R. concinnum* came second, and Dr Jack's *R. rubiginosum* was third.

Class 20, *R. augustinii*, one spray not exceeding 60cm (24in)s in height from the top of the vase. A very fine vase of *R. augustinii* from Exbury took first prize, followed by B.E. Wright's *R. augustinii* 'Electra' in second place.

Class 21, any species of subsects Cinnabarina, Tephropepla or Virgata, one spray no more than 30cm (12in) from top of vase. Exbury won with the only entry, *R. cinnabarinum*.

Class 22, any species of subsects Campylogyna, Genestieriana or Glauca, one spray not exceeding 30cm (12in) in height from the top of the vase. Exbury entered the only two exhibits: *R. glaucophyllum* and *R. charitopes* subsp. *tsangpoense* – first and second respectively.

Class 30, any species of evergreen azalea, one spray not exceeding 45cm (18in) from top of vase. First prize for a lovely, well-staged vase of *R. kiusianum* from Exbury – the only entry.

Mention must be made of the delightful, very large pot of *R. fragrantissimum* exhibited by Mrs Charles Funke of Guildford. The whole plant was covered in sweetly scented flowers in excellent condition. The Show could have been enhanced – by even one Nursery Stand.

Archie Skinner

Main Rhododendron Competition – Hybrids 23–24 April 2002

Was there ever a year that produced such an abundance of flower, so relatively unmolested by frosts, wind or rain? And was there ever a year that displayed bloom so early? Not in any of my gardens in the 30 years that I have been growing rhododendrons. Usually, I am to be found forcing blooms for the Main Competition. This year, I was left wondering what on earth would still be out by the time of the Competition. This year, I was actually holding back my showbench potentials, and cutting from the bush on the day before the show – unheard of.

One would have thought that such a glorious season would have been reflected on the showbench but sadly there were no more participants than last year and nothing ravingly sensational about the quantity or quality of the entries on view – although there were one or two bright spots and a few points of interest:

For the first time, trophy-winners were publicly presented with their cups. The presentations were made by Mr John Hillier, Chairman of the RHS Rhododendron and Camellia Committee. This was a step forward although it would have been better had the presentations been made on the showhall's balcony.

Mrs Ann Hooton of Loxwood, West Sussex made a triumphant return to the Competition after an absence of fourteen years. She won fifteen prizes, including The Loder Cup for the best hybrid, as well as delighting us all with some excellent exhibits. Without doubt, she had lost none of her flair for growing and showing fine rhododendrons.

Exbury, for the first time in decades, did not claim the lion's share of the prizes in the hybrid classes – Mrs Hooton did. The famous garden did, however, treat us to their usual palette of characteristic colour, outstanding among which was the lovely deciduous azalea 'Citron'. Prize-wise, the spoils were fairly evenly distributed among the main competitors, which only goes to prove that anyone can win if you take the trouble to enter. Of the 26 classes, the following caught the eye:

Class 31, six hybrids, one truss of each. For over 25 years, I have been trying to get the better of Exbury in this class. This year I finally succeeded, only to see Mrs Hooton deservedly outdo the both of us. She won with 'Naomi Paris' (a plant of the Naomi grex I am unfamiliar with; could she have meant 'Naomi Stella Maris'?), 'Calfort', 'Taurus', 'Red Glow', 'Roza Stevenson' and 'Colonel Rogers' – an award-winning group that would grace the very best of gardens.

Class 32, for three trusses, saw Mrs Hooton produce another top entry comprising 'Rubicon' and 'Queen of Hearts' (two very good reds) and that gorgeous Exbury yellow, 'Mariloo'. As good as this was, it was pipped by an even better trio from The Isabella Plantation, Richmond, Surrey. This garden showed the rarely seen 'Margaret Bean', an impressive *R. campylocarpum* hybrid, 'Seven Stars' from *R. yakushimanum* × Loderi 'Sir Joseph Hooker' and an attractive entry that was doubtfully described as 'Wally Miller'.

Class 33, any single truss for The Loder Challenge Cup, again proved to be the most popular class in the Competition. It attracted 15 entries and, as mentioned earlier in this account, was won by Mrs Hooton. She showed an exceptionally fine 'Roza Stevenson'. It was not only a good, clear, clean yellow but a truss with unusually large corollas and leaves. One could put this down to good gardening although Mrs Hooton gives the credit to Mr Arthur George, the nurseryman from whom she purchased the plant. Second and third

prizes in this class went to Brian Wright showing the *R. roxieanum* cross 'Blewbury' and 'W.F.H.' that brilliant scarlet hybrid named after W.F. Hamilton, the one-time head gardener of Pylewell Park, Lymington. Not surprisingly, a fourth prize was awarded in this class. It went to Mrs Hooton for her nice *R. thomsonii* hybrid, 'Red Glow'.

Class 34, for large hybrid sprays, was won by Mrs Hooton. She took first prize with 'Roza Stevenson' and then second with her 'Naomi' hybrid. This was far too much for Exbury who were awarded third prize for their good greenish yellow 'Jancio' – an *R. fortunei* hybrid.

Class 35, three hybrids bred and raised in the garden of the exhibitor. This is the class where Exbury come into their own. Unchallenged they won with their well-known 'Naomi Nautilus', 'Crest' and 'Queen of Hearts' and placed their name yet again on The Crosfield Challenge Cup.

Class 36, for Loderi Group trusses, was won by Brian Wright showing a good, clean upright head of 'Loderi King George'. The entry that caught the eye, however, was 'Ilam Cream', the runner-up. Strictly speaking, this was not a Loderi but a Loderi cross, which should have barred it from this class. Notwithstanding, it was real cream in colour with a charming pink flush and obviously a good garden plant. Third place went to Mrs Hooton with 'Loderi Game Chick'.

Although Classes 37 to 47 produced some worthy prize-winning blooms, they have, for the most part, been already covered by this report with the exception, say, of Exbury's excellent 'Biskra', which, with its vermillion, biscuity coloured bells, won Class 47 for subsect. Cinnabarina hybrids; Mrs Hooton's 'Boddaertianum', which dates back to 1863 and nowadays is not much seen – this won Class 46 for subsect. Arborea hybrids; Brian Wright's contrasting 'Teddy Bear', which hardly dates back at all and, as a *R. yakushimanum/ bureavii* cross, was second in Class 45.

Class 50, for Lepidote hybrids, was won by Exbury showing a top-class 'Dora Amateis'. It was closely challenged, however, by a very fresh looking 'Emasculum' flown from Scotland by Dr Robbie Jack. One often wonders what other delights Robbie would bring if he had his own private plane.

As to be expected, the azalea classes were all about pure flower (surely there's a leaf in there somewhere?) Class 55 for evergreens was won by Exbury showing that old favourite 'Hinodegiri'. Second, third and fourth was The Isabella Plantation. Respectively, they showed 'Psyche' – very bright pink – 'Hinodegiri' and 'Orange Beauty'. Class 56, for deciduous types, ended the Competition on a high note with Exbury succeeding with their superb yellow 'Citron' and The Isabella Plantation taking second prize with an attractive yellowish-tangerine plant that appeared to be unnamed.

Brian Wright

Early Camellia Competition
12–13 March 2002

The Camellia exhibits at the Shows are very dependent on the weather, over which the exhibitors have no control. The weather during the winter of 2001–2 was wild and wet, yet the display of spring bloom was superb and amazing growth has since been put on, which hopefully will show off in the spring of 2003. The autumn of 2001 was spectacular for the fine-coloured young foliage and plentiful supply of seeds, which evoked much interest because few people seemed to have seen the seeds previously. Of particular interest, seeds from the 2001 autumn, self-sown, germinated and produced seedlings which have flourished through the 2002 season, very attractive with their rich shiny leaves – who can tell their inheritance or the colour of the flowers to come. Long ago Dr Clifford Parkes gave me a handful of seed from his USA garden, which I grew. He asked me to test the seedlings for cold hardiness in the UK. I need not have worried. Most germinated and produced cultivars that shrugged off the cold. They have grown into beautiful shrubs and display a wide range of flower types, some very beautiful and I really treasure them growing naturally in a woodland setting.

At the 2002 Early Competition, Class 1 (any *C. japonica* spray) attracted six entries and was won by Mr Betteley with a lovely spray of 'Desire' – a beautiful, formal double flower with pale pink petals edged with a deeper pink, a nice upright form. Second came Anne Hooton with 'Joshua Youtz', a very beautiful white with a large, almost formal double flower – it has stood the test of time. Third was Helen Keates who showed a beautiful spray of 'Miss Charlston', an outstanding cultivar with vibrant deep red, semi-double flowers.

Class 2, for any C. × williamsii cultivar spray. First prize was awarded to 'Anticipation' shown by Ann Hooton , a lovely spray with many buds. Second was 'Debbie' shown by Ann Hooton, always a favourite., and third was 'Donation' shown by Mr Betteley, a really fine and well-budded spray.

Class 3, for any hybrid or species spray not eligible for Class 1 or 2. First was Mr Betteley who showed 'Interval' for its first award – a *C. japonica* × *reticulata* with a single, salmon-pink flower. Second place was awarded to 'Royalty' shown by Ann Hooton.

Class 10, for any three single blooms of *C. japonica*. There were three entries and first place was given to Ann Hooton with 'Juno', 'Alba Simplex' and 'Mattie Cole'. Ann Hooton

Fig. 23: Rhododendron kendrickii (pankimense) *flowering at Crarae, Scotland (see p.9).*

Early Camellia Competition at Westminster:
Fig. 24 (left): Camellia *'Mattie Cole' (top),* Camellia *'Alba Simplex' (centre) and* Camellia *'Juno' (bottom) – winner of Class 10 for Ann Hooton (see p.80).*
Fig. 25 (above): The old cultivar Camellia *'Mathotiana Rubra' – an entry by Chatsworth House Trust to Class 17.*
Fig. 26 (below): Camellia *'Lasca Beauty' (right),* Camellia *'Interval' (centre) and* Camellia *'Edith Maggi' (left) – an entry for Class 20, which won first prize for Mr A.W. Simons (see p.82).*

Fig. 27 (above): The City of Swansea entered Class 11 of the Early Rhododendron Competition at Westminster with Rhododendron tantastylum *from Clyne Gardens – a rare plant in cultivation (see p.75).*
Fig. 28 (right): Rhododendron searsiae, *an uncommon member of subsect. Triflora, which won first prize of Class 4 and the Rosa Stevenson Challenge Cup for Exbury Gardens at the Westminster Main Rhododendron Competition (see p.77).*

Fig. 29 (above): Garden at Sherwood, Devon (see p.63).

also took second place with 'Spencer's Pink', 'Henry Turnbull' and 'Splendens' – a lovely flower with pronounced blue veining. Third came Chatsworth House Trust with 'Alba Simplex', 'Jupiter var' and 'Siebold'.

Class 11, for any single-flowered *C. japonica* cultivar. Twelve entries. First was Mr A.W. Simons with 'Ohkan', a quite spectacular flower with a deep pink frill and a newcomer to the Show. Second was Ann Hooton with 'Mattie Cole'. Third was Mrs Jill Totty showing 'Spencers Pink', and fourth was Chatsworth House Trust with 'Jupiter'.

Class 12, for any three semi-double *C. japonica* cultivars, one bloom. Seven entries. First was Sir Edmund de Rothschild presenting 'Adolphe Audusson', 'Dear Jenny' and 'Drama Girl'. Second was Chatsworth House Trust who presented 'Bob Hope' (a really superb bloom), 'Blood of China' and 'Ann Southern'. Third was Ann Hooton with 'Guilio Nuccio', 'Emmett Barnes' and 'Adolphe Audusson'. Fourth was A.W. Simons with 'Lily Pons', 'Blaze of Glory' and 'Wildfire'.

Class 13, for any semi-double cultivar of *C. japonica*. 15 entries. First was 'Easter Mom', a most beautiful camellia and a well-deserved award to Chatsworth House Trust. Second was Mr Betteley with 'Lovelight' and third came Chatsworth House Trust with 'Midnight'.

Class 14, for any three anemone- or peony-formed cultivars. There were seven entries. First prize went to Sir Edmund de Rothschild with 'Strawberry Blonde', 'Debutante' and 'Elegans Champagne'. Second was Chatsworth House Trust with 'Kramers Beauty', 'Elegans' and 'Hawaii'. Third was David Davies with 'Powder Puff', 'Annie Wylam' and 'Mary Costa'.

Class 15, for any anemone- or peony-formed cultivar. Twelve entries. First came Sir Edmund de Rothschild with 'Margaret Davis', a truly lovely example of this beautiful cultivar. Second was Mrs Jill Totty with 'Mary Costa', another outstanding camellia, and third was Ann Hooton with 'R.L. Wheeler'.

Class 16, for any three rose-formed or formal double camellias. There were eight entries. First came David Davis with 'Fimbriata', 'Nuccio's Pearl' and 'Nuccio's Gem'. Second was also David Davis with 'Fimbriata', 'Nuccio's Pearl' and 'Twighlight' – an amazing white pale pink. Third was Chatsworth House Trust with 'Madame Lebois', 'Alba Plena' and 'Grand Sultan'.

Class 17, for any rose-formed or formal double camellia. There were ten entries. First came Chatsworth House Trust with 'Alba Plena', second was Mr Betteley with 'Desire' and third was Chatsworth House Trust with 'Lavinia Maggi' – a very early cultivar from Italy (1858), imbricated tricolour with a very large flower; it has a long and distinguished history and is still enhancing our gardens.

Class 18, for any six cultivars of *C. japonica*, one bloom of each. First came Mr A.W. Simons showing 'Lily Pons', 'Kick-off', 'Wildfire', 'Hawaii', 'Mark Alien' and 'Ohkan', in second place was Ann Hooton presenting 'Splendens', 'Annie Wylam', 'Miss Charlston', 'Guilio Nuccio', 'R.L. Wheeler' and 'Joshua Youtz'. Third came Chatsworth House Trust showing 'R.L. Wheeler', 'Mrs D.W. Davis', 'Latifolia', 'Adolphe Audusson', 'Drama Girl', 'Hakurakuten', and 'Adolphe Audusson'. Fourth was Chatsworth House Trust showing 'William Bartlett', 'Marguérite Gouillon', 'Bob Hope', 'Her Majesty', 'Grand Sultan' and 'Alba Plena'.

Class 19, for any three cultivars of *C. japonica*, one bloom of each. There were eleven entries. First was Ann Hooton with 'Joshua

Youtz', 'Margaret Davis' and 'Flowerwood'. Second came David Davis with 'Lady Campbell', 'Diana's Charm' and 'Mary Costa'. In third place came Chatsworth House Trust showing 'Gullio Nuccio', 'Dixie Knight' and 'Jupiter var', and in fourth was Helene Keates with 'Miss Charlston', 'Lavinia Maggi' and 'Debutante'.

Class 20, for any three hybrids, one bloom of each. There were eight entries. First was A.W. Simons with 'Lasca Beauty', 'Interval' and 'Edith Maggi'. Second came Ann Hooton with 'Royalty', 'Lasca Beauty' and 'Dr C. Parkes'. Third was Mr Betteley with 'Valentine Day', 'Miss Tulare' and 'Otto Hopfer'.

Class 21, for any *C. reticulata* hybrid of which one parent is *C. × williamsii* or *C. saluenensis*. There were six entries. First was Chatsworth House Trust with 'Francie L'. Second came Anne Hooton with 'Francie L', and third was Mr Betteley 'Valley Knudsen'.

Class 22, for any Reticulata camellia species or hybrid. There were 14 entries. How can you select the best from all such wonderful blooms? First was Mr Betteley with 'Miss Tulare', second came David Davis with 'Harold L Paige', Mr Betteley was third with 'Lila Naff', and Chatsworth House Trust were fourth with 'Captain Rawes'. Highly Commended – David Davis with 'Harold L Paige'.

Class 23, for any three *C. × williamsii*, one bloom of each. There were six entries. First prize was awarded to Ann Hooton with 'Anticipation', 'Daintiness' and 'Les Jury'. Second came Mrs Jill Totty with 'Elizabeth Anderson', unknown and 'Mirage', and Chatsworth House Trust came third with 'Jury's Yellow', 'Muskoka' and 'Eldorado'.

Class 24, for any single *C. × williamsii*. There were seven entries. First came

Chatsworth House Trust with 'Francis Hanger', second came Anne Hooton with 'Mary Larcom', and Chatsworth House Trust were third with 'Ruby Bells'.

Class 25, for any semi-double *C. × williamsii*. There were six entries. First came Ann Hooton showing 'Daintiness', and second was Chatsworth House Trust showing 'Glenn's Orbit', a lovely flower but seldom sown. In third was A.W. Simons showing 'Nightrider', an outstanding, dark red bloom.

Class 26, for any peony- or anemone-formed *C. × williamsii*. There were tens entries. Chatsworth House Trust came first with 'Debbie', Ann Hooton was second with 'Anticipation', A.W. Simons was third with 'Ballet Queen' and Helene Keates was fourth with 'Debbie'.

Class 27, for any hybrid other than of *C. reticulata* or *C. × williamsii*. There were six entries. David Davis gained first and second prizes, each time with 'Nicky Crisp', Sir Edmund de Rothschild was third with 'Freedom Bell'.

Class 28, for any yellow cultivar, one bloom. There were three entries. First came Chatsworth House Trust showing 'Jury's Yellow', second was 'Barbara Griffith' with 'Jury's Yellow', and third was Helen Keates also showing 'Jury's Yellow'.

Class 29, for any species, one bloom. There were four entries. First prize was awarded to A.W. Simons with *C. transnokoensis*, a tiny, single white camellia with lovely apricot-coloured young foliage. Second prize also went to A.W. Simons with *C. forrestii*.

Cicely Perring

Main Camellia Competition 2002
This competition was cancelled because of the funeral of Her Majesty the Queen Mother.

Camellia japonica 'Black Tie'

AM 13 March 2001 as a hardy flowering plant for exhibition. Raised by S C Walden jr, USA. Exhibited by Dr J A Smart, Marwood Hill, Marwood, Barnstaple, Devon EX31 4EB. The opening flower passes through a distinctive "rose-bud" stage when the outer petals are open and the inner ones form a neat cone. Flower miniature formal double, 70mm diameter; petals *c*.50, red (45A), outer 35 × 25mm, inner 25 × 10mm. Leaves broadly elliptic, shiny, dark green. Specimen and transparency in Herb. Hort. Wisley.

Magnolia 'Lois'

AM 25 April 2000 as a hardy flowering plant for exhibition. Exhibited by M Foster, White House Farm, Ivy Hatch, Sevenoaks, Kent TN15 0NN. This magnolia hybrid between *M. acuminata* and *M. acuminata* × *denudata* was raised at Brooklyn Botanic Garden and first flowered in 1996. It appears to exhibit the arboreal growth habit of *M. acuminata* but with the flower shape and petal size approaching *M. denudata*. The open cup-shaped flowers, 12–14cm diameter, have 8–9 obovate tepals, 5–7 × 3.5–4cm, pale yellow (8C-D) inside, (8B) outside, but paler at the edges and slightly flushed green at the base. Anthers golden yellow, near (162C). Specimen in Herb. Hort. Wisley.

Magnolia sprengeri 'Burncoose'

AM 14 March 2000 as a hardy flowering plant for exhibition. Exhibited by C H Williams, Burncoose Nurseries, Gwennap, Redruth, Cornwall TR16 6BJ. This cultivar arose from a self-fertilised, hand-pollinated seedling of 'Diva', selected for its darker richer, more purple-coloured flowers. It was raised by Arnold Dance at Burncoose Garden and first flowered in 1972. It forms a magnificent tree with upward curving branches arising from the base. The flowers reach 22cm in diameter, with 10–14 obovate tepals, 9–13 × 4.5–7cm. Buds deep purplish red (Red-Purple Group 61A-B) opening slightly paler (64B) on the outside, shading darker at the base and paler purplish pink on the inside (74B) becoming darker towards the margins of the tepals. Undehisced anthers pink 61A. Specimen in Herb. Hort. Wisley.

Magnolia 'Sweetheart'

AM 18 March 1997 as a hardy flowering plant for exhibition. Exhibited by M Foster, White House Farm, Ivy Hatch, Sevenoaks, Kent TN15 0NN. This plant which arose as a seedling of 'Caerhays Belle', was raised by Peter Cave in New Zealand. It forms an upright and vigorous early flowering tree. Flowers scented, globose, to 19cm diameter but up to 30cm when fully open. Tepals *c*.12, broad obovate to obovate, outer 15 × 8cm, inner 12 × 5.5cm, outside of tepals purplish pink (near 66D to 65A-B) deepening at base on outside, white to very pale pink (near 65D) on inside. Leaves not present at flowering. Specimen in Herb. Hort. Wisley.

Rhododendron dendrocharis

CC&H 4012 PC 28 April 2001, as a hardy flowering plant for exhibition. Exhibited by Mr and Mrs P Hurst, 9 North Rise, Greenfield, Saddleworth, Oldham OL3 7ED. Stems and petioles covered in dense, long, slightly flexuous rather rigid hairs. Leaves elliptic, with blades up to 16 × 7.5mm, obtuse and apiculate, margins decurved, glabrous above, lower surface with numerous, but still distinct, small, amber-coloured scales, and with a few rigid hairs at margin towards base. Flowers solitary; calyx 7mm long, deeply lobed, the lobes, oblong, obtuse, ciliate; base of calyx with colourless scales and very short hairs, corolla *c.*29 × 40mm, open funnel-campanulate, light purplish pink (73C) with variable pink flushing, not scaly; stamens 10; style as long as stamens, declinate. Specimen in Herb. Hort. Wisley.

Rhododendron 'Mrs Lionel de Rothschild'

FCC 21 May 2001, as a hardy flowering plant for exhibition. Probably raised by A Waterer. Exhibited by E de Rothschild, Exbury Gardens, Exbury, Southampton, Hampshire SO45 1AZ. Truss of *c.*18 flowers, 160mm in diameter. Corolla openly funnel-shaped, 40 × 70mm, 5-lobed, white, lobes edged with very thin purplish pink line, prominent dorsal blotch of contiguous red-purple (59B) flecks on upper lobe extending slightly to lateral lobes. Stamens 10–11, 35mm, included; filaments white, slightly pubescent at base; anthers pale pinkish beige. Style 30mm, white, faintly green and slightly pubescent at base; ovary dark green, glandular. Calyx very irregular with some lobes to 10mm, reddish purple (59C). Pedicel 40–60mm, reddish purple (59C). Leaves oblong, 170 × 50mm, scattered black hair-bases along midrib on underside. Specimen and transparency in Herb.Hort.Wisley.

Rhododendron 'Ken Janeck'

AM 21 May 2001, as a hardy flowering plant for exhibition. Raised by K Janeck. Exhibited by Crown Estate Commissioners, The Great Park, Windsor, Berkshire SL4 2HT. Seedling of *R. yakushimanum*. Rounded truss of *c.*12 flowers, 160mm in diameter. Corolla 50 × 70mm, funnel-campanulate, 5-lobed, white with faint pink flushing confined to exterior midrib of some lobes, dorsal blotch 20 × 20mm of diffuse, pale green (145A) spots. Stamens 10, 35mm, included; filaments white, pubescent at base; anthers pale brown. Style 40mm, greenish white, flushed pink at apex; ovary dark green, pubescent. Calyx insignificant, to 3mm, pubescent. Pedicel 50–60mm, green with faint red flushing, pubescent. Leaves oblong-elliptic, 120 × 35mm, underside with dense, pale brown indumentum.

PHOTOGRAPHIC COMPETITION

A decent number of entries was again received this year, although none under the "spouse's category". First place and the prize of £25 went to Mr J. G. Rees with a study of *Magnolia sieboldii* taken in his own garden. Second was Mr C. Waddington with his picture of *Rhododendron lindleyi*. Third was Dr G. Hargreaves with a picture of the Westonbirt *Magnolia sprengeri* var. *diva*. All three photos, as is customary, are printed in this issue (see figs 20–22). Congratulations to the winners, and thanks as always to all those members who took the trouble to submit entries. Please keep on trying.   *Philip Evans*

RHS Rhododendron and Camellia Committee

Chairman
J G Hillier, c/o Hillier Nurseries, Ampfield House, Ampfield, Romsey, Hants SO51 9PA

Vice-Chairman
J T Gallagher, Oldfield, 29 Moorlands Road, Verwood, Dorset BH31 6PD

Secretary
M Grant, RHS Garden Wisley

Members
Lord Aberconway, VMH, Bodnant, Tal-y-Cafn, Colwyn Bay, Clwyd LL28 5RE
B Archibold, Starveacre, Dalwood, Axminster, East Devon EX13 7HH
The Hon. Edward Boscawen, The Garden House, High Beeches Lane, Handcross, Sussex
    RH17 6HQ
C Fairweather, The Garden Centre, High Street, Beaulieu, Hampshire SO42 7YR
M Flanagan, Verderers, Wick Road, Englefield Green, Egham, Surrey TW20 3AE
M Foster, White House Farm, Ivy Hatch, Sevenoaks, Kent TN15 0NN
A F George, Hydon Nurseries, Hydon Heath, Godalming, Surrey GU8 4AZ
Dr R H L Jack, Edgemoor, Loch Road, Lanark ML11 9BG
D G Millais, Crosswater Farm, Churt, Farnham, Surrey GU10 2JN
M Pharoah, Marwood Hill, Marwood, Barnstaple, Devon EX31 4EB
M C A Robinson, Hindhead Lodge, Priory Road, Forest Row, E Sussex RH18 5JF
A Simons, Wingfield House, 11 Brinsmade Road, Ampthill, Bedfordshire
A V Skinner, MBE, 2 Frog Firle Cottage, Alfriston, nr Polegate, E Sussex BN26 5TT
M O Slocock, VMH, Knap Hill Nursery, Barrs Lane, Knaphill, Woking, Surrey
    GU21 2JW
Major T le M Spring-Smyth, 1 Elcombe's Close, Lyndhurst, Hants SO43 7DS
O R Staples, 10 Close Gardens, Tetbury, Glos GL8 8DU
C Tomlin, Starborough Nursery, Starborough Road, Marsh Green, Edenbridge, Kent
    TN8 5RB
Miss J Trehane, Church Cottage, Hampreston, Wimborne, Dorset BH21 7LX
C H Williams, Burncoose Nurseries, Gwennap, Redruth, Cornwall TR16 6BJ
F J Williams, Caerhays Castle, Gorran, St Austell, Cornwall PL26 6LY

RHS Rhododendron, Camellia and Magnolia Group

— 🖤 —

Officers

Chairman Mr Maurice C FOSTER, White House Farm, Ivy Hatch, Sevenoaks, Kent TN15 0NN (Tel: 01732 810634, Fax: 01732 810553)

Hon. Treasurer Mr Martin D C GATES, 12 Marlborough Road, Chandlers Ford, Eastleigh, Hants SO53 5DH (Tel: 023 8025 2843)

Hon. Secretary Mrs Josephine M WARREN, Netherton, Buckland Monachorum, Yelverton, Devon PL20 7NL (Tel/fax: 01822 854022, email: WarrenJosephine@aol.com)

Hon. Membership Secretary Mrs Miranda Gunn, Ramster, Chiddingfold, Surrey GU8 4SN (Tel: 01428 644422, Fax: 01428 658345, email: ramster@bigfoot.com)

Hon. Yearbook Editor Mr Philip D EVANS, West Netherton, Drewsteignton, Devon EX6 6RB (Tel/fax: 01647 281285, email: philip.d.evans@talk21.com)

Hon. Bulletin Editor Mr John A. Rawling, The Spinney, Station Road, Woldingham, Surrey CR3 7DD (Tel: 01883 653341, email: jr.eye@virgin.net)

Hon. Tours Organiser Mrs Valerie ARCHIBOLD, Starveacre, Dalwood, Axminster, Devon EX13 7HH (Tel/fax: 01404 881221 – phone first)

Committee Members

Mr David N FARNES, 5 Pine View (off Deerlands Road), Ashgate, Chesterfield, Derbyshire S40 4DN (Tel: 01246 272105)

Mr John D HARSANT, Newton House, Wall Lane, Heswell, Wirral, Merseyside L60 8NF (Tel: 0151 342 3664, Fax: 0151 348 4015, email: john@harsant.uk.com)

Dr R H L JACK, Edgemoor, Loch Road, Lanark ML11 9BG (Tel: 01555 663021)

Miss Cicely E PERRING, Watermill House, Watermill Lane, Pett, E Sussex TN35 4HY (Tel: 01424 812103)

Mr Alastair T STEVENSON, Appledore, Upton Bishop, Ross-on-Wye, Herefordshire HR9 7UL (Tel: 01989 780285, Fax: 01989 780591, email: alastairstevenson@tiscali.co.uk

Mr Ivor T STOKES, Pantcoch, Carmel, Llanelli, Dyfed SA14 7SG (Tel: 01269 844048)

Branch Chairmen

International Mr Michael JURGENS, The Old House, Silchester, Reading, Berkshire RG7 2LU (Tel: 01189 700240, Fax: 01189 701682)

New Forest Mr Christopher FAIRWEATHER, The Garden Centre, High Street, Beaulieu, Hants SO42 7YR (Tel: 01590 612307, Fax: 01590 612519, email: chrisfairweather@waitrose.com)

Norfolk Mrs J M IDIENS, Beaconswood, Roman Camp, Sandy Lane, West Runton, Cromer, Norfolk NR27 9ND (Tel: 01263 837779, email: idiens@email.msn.com)

North Wales and Northwest Mr C E J BRABIN, Rosewood, Puddington Village, Neston
    CH64 5SS (Tel: 0151 353 1193)
Peak District Mr David N FARNES, 5 Pine View (off Deerlands Road), Ashgate,
    Chesterfield, Derbyshire, S40 4DN (Tel: 01246 272105)
Southeast Dr M L A ROBINSON, Hindhead Lodge, Priory Road, Forest Row, E Sussex
    RH18 5JF (Tel: 01342 822745, email: mlarob@hotmail.com)
Southwest Mrs Margaret MILES, Trewollack, St Mawes, Truro, Cornwall TR2 5AD
    (Tel/fax: 01326 270229)
Ulster Mr Patrick FORDE, Seaforde, Downpatrick, Co Down BT30 8PG
    (Tel: 01396 811225, Fax: 01396 811370)
Wessex Mrs Miranda GUNN, Ramster, Petworth Road, Chiddingfold, Surrey GU8 4SN
    (Tel: 01428 644422, Fax: 01428 658345, email: Ramster@bigfoot.com)
Convenor of Group Seed Bank Mr Tony WESTON, Whitehills, Newton Stewart, Scotland
    DG8 6SL (Tel: 01671 402049, Fax: 01671 403106, email: caweston@rhodo.demon.uk)
Yearbook Archivist Mrs Pam HAYWARD, Woodtown, Sampford Spiney, Yelverton, Devon
    PL20 6LJ (Tel/fax: 01822 852122, email: WoodtownPam@aol.com)

Membership: for details of Membership please contact the Hon. Membership Secretary
Website address: www.rhs.org.uk/rhsgroups/memb.asp

INDEX

Rhododendrons & Azaleas

FOR THE CONNOISSEUR FROM **LODER PLANTS**

MAIL ORDER, PLANT CENTRE & EXPORT. TEL:**01403-891412** FAX **891336**.
SEND 2 x1ST STAMPS FOR AVAILABILITY LIST OR VIST OUR WEBSITE AT **www.rhododendrons.com**
OPEN BY APPOINTMENT ONLY. THIS IS SO WE CAN GIVE YOU OUR UNDIVIDED ATTENTION & ADVICE
(OVER 1000 HYBRIDS, SPECIES AND AZALEAS, EVERGREEN OR DECIDUOUS, EARLY OR LATE
FLOWERING, SCENTED) & ACERS, CAMELLIA'S, MAGNOLIAS AND MANY OTHER CHOICE PLANTS

JUST SOUTH OF

We're sure you'll enjoy a day at Leonardslee so much you'll invest in a season ticket and return again and again! The many miles of walks provide never ending delights and a changing landscape throughout the seasons. There are plenty of quiet spots where you can sit and enjoy one of England's greenest and most pleasant landscapes. The walks extend round the peaceful lakes and waterfalls where wildlife thrives.

Escape from the busy world in Leonardslee's tranquil 240 acres and enjoying the high variety of natural habitats. Watch the large carp in the Waterfall lake and glimpse wallabies and deer in their idyllic setting. Don't miss the Alpine House and Bonsai Exhibition, with lunch or tea in the Clock Tower Restaurant, and before you leave, browse around the good selection of plants for sale at the nursery.

Enjoy the Autumnal glory of Leonardslee where Maples and deciduous Azaleas take on their dramatic shades against the golds and russets of fine woodland trees. Liquidambars, Hickories and Tupelos provide shades of copper and gold. From mid-September until late October the colours change every week. The end of the season can be as dramatic as the beginning

LOWER BEEDING, HORSHAM, W.SUSSEX RH13 6PP. TEL: 01403 891212 FAX: 891305

EXBURY GARDENS & STEAM RAILWAY

Discover world famous displays of rhododendrons, azaleas and camellias within a 200-acre woodland garden. Let our new $12^{1}/_{4}$" gauge Steam Railway take you on a magical 20 minute journey over a bridge, through a tunnel and across a pond in the newly created Summer Lane Garden. With an excellent plant centre, gift shop and catering facilities, Exbury offers a truly memorable day out!

OPEN SPRING, SUMMER AND AUTUMN

20 minutes from M27, J2
4 miles from Beaulieu

FOR FURTHER INFORMATION RING
(023) 8089 9422
or (023) 8089 1203

WWW.EXBURY.CO.UK

GLENDOICK™
GARDENS LIMITED

Glendoick, Perth PH2 7NS, Scotland

RETAIL NURSERY OF THE YEAR 2002
(Nurseryman and Garden Centre Awards)

Phone: 01738 860 205 Fax: 01738 860 630 Email: sales@glendoick.com

70 page colour catalogue and colour price list available now. Plants can be collected or sent worldwide. October-1st April. Send £2 for a copy.

See hundreds of plants in full colour on our website www.glendoick.com

EXCITING ITEMS THIS YEAR INCLUDE:
R. cephalanthum Nmaiense Group fist ever collection by Kenneth Cox, *R. pudorosum* CER, first new introduction since Ludlow & Sherriff from Tsari, Tibet. *R. dekatanum* L&S: a beautiful yellow species (formerly sold as *R. sulphureum* aff). Stunning new azalea hybrids: the huge yellow orange 'Arenson's Gem' and the scented 'Fragrant Star'. New Glendoick hybrid azaleas: 'Glendoick Crimson', 'Glendoick Dream, 'Glendoick Glacier' (protected varieties may not be commercially propagated). Lots of recent species introductions from China and Tibet such as *R. oligocarpum* and *R. ochraceum*, *R. rothschildii*, *R. × populare*, *R. latouchiae*, *R. sinofalconeri* etc.

We also grow all sorts of wonderful plants such as Camellias, *Sorbus, Epigea, Nomocharis, Meconopsis*, Lilies, *Kalmia latifolia, Omphalogramma*, etc etc.

TWO NEW BOOKS AVAILABLE THIS YEAR:
The Encyclopedia of Rhododendron Species (2nd Edition) by Peter A. Cox & Kenneth N.E. Cox Due to popular demand, a Second Edition has been published featuring all of the original material as well as three additional pages featuring new species introduced since 1997. These include R. monanthum, R. platypodum, R. miniatum, R. gongshanense and several others. Price £75 plus postage & packing (approx. £8).
Frank Kingdon Ward's Riddle of the Tsangpo Gorges (New edition) Edited by Kenneth Cox, Antique Collector's Club, 2001. Original text by Frank Kingdon Ward, edited by Kenneth Cox. Additional material by Kenneth Cox, Ken Storm Jr. and Ian Baker. Price £35 plus postage & packing (approx. £6–7).

Books can be ordered over the phone with a credit card.

In Preparation: Peter Cox and Sir Peter Hutchison – Memoirs of 37 years of Plant hunting. 100s of photographs.